ARTISANS OF THE PUNJAB

A Study of Social Change in Historical Perspective (1849-1947)

ARTISANS OF THE PUNJAB

A Study of Social Change in Historical Perspective (1849-1947)

HARISH C. SHARMA

MANOHAR
1996

The publication of this book has been financially supported by the Indian Council of Historical Research, and the responsibility for the facts or opinions expressed is entirely of the author and not of the Council.

ISBN 81-7304-127-X

First Published 1996

Published by
Ajay Kumar Jain
Manohar Publishers & Distributors
2/6, Ansari Road, Daryaganj
New Delhi - 110002

Laser typeset by
A J Software Publishing Co. Pvt. Ltd.
305, Durga Chambers,
1333, D.B. Gupta Road,
Karol Bagh, New Delhi - 110005

Printed at
Rajkamal Electric Press
G.T. Karnal Road
Delhi

TO
MY FATHER
PT. BEHARI LAL SHARMA

Contents

Preface

Interest in social history, developed in India after independence, is largely due to the growing awareness and concern for tracing the roots of contemporary social problems and economic backwardness of the country particularly the lowly evaluated castes. The socially and economically backward sections particularly the lowly evaluated castes forming a substantial chunk of Indian population have been the focus of attention. The present work is an attempt to comprehend the position of the artisan castes in the British Punjab where they formed nearly one-fifth of the total population.

The book, the revised version of my doctoral thesis approved by Guru Nanak Dev University, Amritsar in 1986, is a study of the artisans in their response to the changing social, economic, and political conditions under British rule in the Punjab. The terms of reference for the treatment of the subject are: origins of change; channels and mechanism of its diffusion; and the nature and consequences of change. In seven chapters the study takes into account the position of the artisans in the traditional socio-economic, technological and educational developments under colonial rule having a direct or indirect bearing on the artisans; and occupational mobility leading to new patterns of social relationships within an artisan caste and with others. The new patterns of social relations eventually led towards the emergence of socio-political organizations among the lower castes leading in some cases also to political articulation.

The processes that affect people and the traditional institutions are not possible to be studied over a short period, especially when the diffusion of change and the response of the people is exceedingly slow. This, at any rate, is true of the artisans of the Punjab. This work, therefore, covers nearly a hundred years of British rule.

The Punjab for the purpose of this study means the territories which remained under direct administration of the British from 1849 to 1947 and, therefore, it does not, include the princely states and the territories of North Western Frontier Province and Delhi which were separated from the Punjab in 1901 and 1911 respectively. The hill districts and the districts of eastern and western Punjab in their pattern of agriculture, composition of the agrarian society and the level of dependence on the village artisans were different from one another. In the districts of central Punjab plains—nearly half of the British Punjab—the framework of the agrarian society of which the village artisans formed an integral part, pattern of agriculture and traditions were broadly homogeneous. The conclusions are, therefore, mainly on the basis of the data related to this area.

The framework and methods of the allied disciplines, particularly sociology and social anthropology, have been found extremely useful for this study. To trace the pattern of new social relations the interview method was applied and the responses of about one hundred persons selected from various districts of central Punjab, including those who had migrated from Pakistan after partition, were processed and analyzed. The results thus obtained support the hypothesis that readjustments in social relations of different castes following spatial and occupational change, and changes in the general socio-economic context were going on. In fact, in terms of new social relations it is possible to see broad continuity between the period before and after independence.

I am indebted to the people of the artisan castes of several villages of the districts of Amritsar, Jalandhar, Hoshiarpur, and Gurdaspur, over a score of whom were from the districts of Montgomery, Lyallpur, and Gujranwala (now in Pakistan). They tolerated my lengthy interviews and my insistence on detail in the course of my field work. Meetings with them have helped me immensely in clarifying my ideas.

I am happy to acknowledge with thanks the help I received

from several institutions, particularly the National Archives of India and the Nehru Memorial Museum and Library, New Delhi; Indian Institute of Advanced Study, Shimla; the Punjab State Archives, Patiala; the Haryana State Archives, the Panjab University Library, Dwarka Dass Library, all at Chandigarh; the Sikh History Research Library, Khalsa College, Bhai Gurdas Library and the libraries of the departments of History, Sociology and Economics of Guru Nanak Dev University, at Amritsar.

I am thankful to the Indian Council of Historical Research, New Delhi for awarding me the Contingent and Travel Grant and the Publication Subsidy for the completion and publication of this work.

I am grateful to Shri Ramesh C. Jain for taking keen interest in the publication of the work.

I wish, I could find adequate words to express my deep sense of gratitude to Professor Indu Banga for all the support and guidance that I received during my doctoral research. I continued to get the benefit of her advice in the preparation of the present version. I shall always remain indebted to Professor J.S. Grewal for initiating me into the field of historical research. I am grateful to him for taking a keen interest in my work and encouraging me at all the stages of this study.

To thank Radha, my wife and colleague, for all the informal discussions and critical reminders, academic and otherwise, is to underplay the significance of her role in the final shape of this study. My little daughters Divya and Sumedha too deserve a word of appreciation for their patience and tolerance.

Shimla
May 1993

Harish C. Sharma

CHAPTER ONE

Introduction

In the whole range of studies on the socio-economic history of the Punjab under colonial rule the dominant concern of historians, sociologists and social anthropologists has been with the study of agrarian social structure. They have focussed particularly on the landlords, peasant-proprietors, tenants and money-lenders who were undergoing rearrangements and readjustments under new conditions. Among them, the British administrators and the scholars like S.S. Thorburn, H. Calvert and Malcolm Darling were mainly concerned with the land revenue administration, rural indebtedness and transfer of land to non-agriculturists. After 1947 scholars continued to study the society and economy of the Punjab under colonial rule almost on the same pattern.[1] However, the artisans or the handicraftsmen specializing in their inherited skills and working in family groups or as individuals in villages and towns and cities forming about one-fifth of the village society have been the last to receive serious attention from historians and other social scientists.

In the traditional socio-economic set-up the artisans were an integral part of the village society. Their manufacturing activity and agricultural production were complimentary to each other. They manufactured agricultural implements, clothes and provided services and in return received a certain share of crops under the arrangement synonymous to the traditional system *jajmani,* called *sepidari* in the Punjab. The manufacturing activity of the artisans was important for the sustenance of the urban economy as well. The artisans were

[1] See for instance Barrler (1966), Dungen (1972) and Domin (1977).

identified by their castes corresponding to their inherited skills. Important among them were the blacksmiths or the Lohars, carpenters or the Tarkhans, weavers or the Julahas, potters or the Kumhars, leather-workers or the Chamars and Mochis and goldsmiths or the Sunars. In the changed socio-economic conditions under the British complimentarity between the manufacturing activity in villages and processes of agricultural production was disrupted. This was followed by occupational mobility and changes in the social and economic conditions among the artisan castes which led to the emergence of new patterns of social relations among the artisan castes themselves and with others which eventually got articulated in socio-political organizations such as the Ad-Dharm Mandal.

Among the scholars who have dealt with the socio-economic position of the artisans at some length may be mentioned: Tom G. Kessinger, Himadri Banerjee, P.H.M. van den Dungen, Satish Saberwal and Ethne K. Marenco. The two early attempts by G.S. Chhabra and B.S. Saini to study the general social and economic history of the Punjab, however, refer to the artisans only in passing.

The works of Chhabra and Saini present generalized narratives of aspects of the society and economy of the Punjab respectively in the late nineteenth and the early twentieth century. Saini's work was published about thirteen years after Chhabra's, but both of them follow more or less the same plan and the same approach to study social and economic condition of the people of the Punjab. They begin their account with the life and manners of the people, take into account social institutions, customs and religious beliefs, narrate developments in education, agriculture, industries, trade, communications, finance, and finally the overall condition in terms of the 'prosperity' of the people. These works do not analyse the impact of these developments on different sections of the Punjabi society or the responses of the people. Nor do these works present an integrated picture of social and economic change under colonial rule. They are, however, useful in presenting an overview of the general social and economic condition of the Punjab under British rule.

Himadri Banerjee's work on the Punjab during the second half of the nineteenth century is an attempt to study 'some of the major influences to which the agrarian society of the Punjab was exposed'. The study takes into account colonization following irrigation projects, commercialization of agriculture, land revenue administration, rural credit and land alienation and the changing pattern of relations between tenants and the *zamindars.* There is also a chapter on the *kamins,* which gives useful information on the Kumhars, Lohars, Tarkhans and the Chamars in terms of their general condition, their income and the mode and amount of their remuneration. Banerjee has drawn heavily upon the land revenue settlement reports and the sources like the surveys of prices and wages, district gazetteers and the records in the office of the Financial Commissioner, Punjab. He relates the acquisition of land by the artisan castes during the second half of the nineteenth century with the commercialization of agriculture. But the study of the effects of the changes in agrarian society on the socio-economic condition of the artisan castes in specific terms does not fall within the purview of Banerjee's otherwise valuable work.

P.H.M. van den Dungen in a section of his article has dealt with the trend toward acquisition of land by the artisans during the British rule. A continuation from the earlier period, this process was accelerated under the Raj. Dungen takes up the cases of the Lohars and the Tarkhans who changed their occupations and became agriculturists during the second half of the nineteenth century. The settlement and assessment reports are the major sources of his information.

Sociologists and social anthropologists have also taken some interest in studying change among the lower evaluated caste groups. Satish Saberwal studies social mobility among the Balmiks, the Ramgarhias and the Ad-Dharmis in an urban context. Saberwal's work is divided into three major parts: (a) historical, spatial and theoretical frameworks; (b) historical setting and the mobility domains of the Balmiks, Ramgarhias and the Ad-Dharmis; and (c) strategies and consequences of change, that is politicization, intra-caste and inter-caste relations. The achievements of the three groups after 1947 have been traced back to the late nineteenth and early twentieth century. Despite the inadequacy of source material, which obliges Saberwal to be often speculative in his analysis, his *Mobile Men* is a welcome contribution to historical sociology.

Tom G. Kessinger has exploded the myth of the dearth of source materials for studying social change in rural areas. Kessinger takes into account demographic change, changes in agriculture and industries, and their cumulative effects on the village life. His *Vilyatpur 1848-1968* is based on wide ranging source material, including the village records, census and settlement reports and other official and unofficial contemporary accounts. *Vilyatpur* is a case study of social and economic change in a village of the Jalandhar Doab in the Punjab and is perhaps the only work of its kind studying society in the region in a micro-setting and over an extended period of time. It takes into account the processes like the effects of the introduction of technology, commercialization of agriculture, migration from rural to urban areas and urbanization. The author deals with the agrarian society composed of various categories of people belonging to different castes and classes, including the artisans, who served the agriculturists under the *sep* system. Kessinger studies change in depth by employing the case study method of sociologists and the anthropologist's method of measuring change between generations. He supplements these by field work and interviews. However, in depth analysis of occupational mobility and its consequences for the artisans falls outside the purview of Kessinger's work.

Ethne K. Marenco, also a social anthropolgist by training, studies social change in the Punjab during the nineteenth and twentieth centuries, and focuses on the response of the Sikhs to the opportunities provided by British rule. This work studies the bearing of the changes in the Punjab under the British on the changes in occupations among the Sikhs, including the artisans. The artisan castes have been taken up in one chapter as a part of the discussion of the transformation of Sikh society in which the menials and untouchables were numerically as important as the agriculturist and trading castes. In due course the Sikh society in the Punjab was 'transformed' from a society based on caste to a society of entrepreneurs. It is, however, not easily possible to follow all the threads in Marenco's argument or to accept her contention that there was corporate caste mobility among the Sikh artisan and menial castes. The work is based mainly on the census reports.

II

The sources used by Marenco, Kessinger, Banerjee, Dungen, Chhabra and Saini are many and varied like the administration reports, census reports, settlement reports, district gazetteers and the revenue administration reports. The usefulness of the census reports for the study of the artisans, however, comes out only in Marenco's work. No other scholar utilizes the rich data provided by the census reports of the Punjab which, when supplemented by other sources, such as the monographs and reports of industries, village surveys and the publications of the Board of Economic Inquiry, enable us to study social change among different castes and occupational groups under British rule.

At any rate, the census reports remain the most important source of our information on the artisan castes and professions. The first census in the Punjab was taken in 1855, followed by that of 1868, and then from 1881 regular decennial censuses started, and the process continued unobstructed upto 1941. However, the census of 1941 could not be taken properly due to the government's preoccupation with World War II and is altogether silent about the artisan castes and their professions.[2] The report of 1855 is no better, whereas the census of 1868 contains some information only

[2] The general data consisting of the statement of population, its religion-wise distribution and urban-rural proportions, however, were compiled: See *Census Punjab 1941*.

on their district-wise distribution. Thus, for the study of social change among the artisans of the Punjab the census reports from 1881 to 1931 remain our major source. During this period elaborate arrangements were made to collect and verify the census data.[3]

Besides presenting the district-wise distribution of the artisans in accordance with their castes and professions, these reports throw some light on their socio-economic conditions. Part I of each report contains information on the general conditions of the people of the province during the period intervening the census and part II provides detailed tables of population according to religion, caste, occupations, education and age-groups as well as the distribution of population over the administrative divisions and districts of the Punjab.

The census report of 1881 is particularly valuable for throwing light on the position of artisans in the socio-economic set-up of the Punjab. The most important part of this report from our view point is its chapter on castes and tribes later published under the title *Punjab Castes*. It is an account of 'The Races, Castes and Tribes and the People' divided in to six parts: (i) concept of caste and tribe; (ii) Biloch and Pathan tribes; (iii) Jats and Rajputs; (iv) minor landowning castes; (v) religious, professional and trading castes; and (vi) the vagrant, menial and artisan castes. The census reports of 1911, 1921, and 1931 are especially helpful in tracing the occupations of the artisan castes. There is a separate table entitled 'Occupations of Selected Castes and

[3] The census data were collected and verified in two stages. It was announced beforehand about the particular evening on which the census was to be taken and the presence of all family members in the house was expected. This was called the preliminary census. Final lists were prepared after verifying the data collected earlier. The verification was done on the spot after one week of the preliminary census. For the purpose of the collection of data each district was sub-divided into blocks, circles and charges. Each block consisted of 500 persons, a group of several blocks made a circle and a number of circles formed a charge. The questions by enumerators were related to religion, caste, mother tongue, district or province of birth, occupation and literacy: see *Census Punjab 1891*, pt I, 11.

Tribes', which enumerated the members of artisan castes engaged in various categories of professions, such as agriculture, mining, industry, trade, transport and government service. The number of those who returned themselves as engaged in their traditional caste occupations is given separately. This table is also helpful in forming a fair idea of occupational mobility among the artisans.[4]

The land revenue settlement reports of various districts of the Punjab also take notice of the artisans and menials.[5] These reports refer to them according to their castes which is extremely useful in understanding their position in the traditional socio-economic set-up during the late nineteenth century. The settlement officers even noticed the artisans shifting to other occupations, especially agriculture, in different capacities. The settlement and assessment reports of the period also take notice of the changing relations between the agriculturists and the artisans.

The first series of the district gazetteers of the Punjab, prepared in 1883-84, too contain a good deal of information on the artisans serving under *sepi* arrangements and also on those who worked outside this framework.[6] These gazetteers throw considerable light on the remuneration of the *sepis* and help us form some idea of their general economic condition. The data given in the appendices are largely based on the census report of 1881 and the annual reports on internal and external trade. By putting together the information provided

[4] The table 'Occupations of Selected Castes and Tribes' includes thirteen occupational categories: the exploitation of the surface of the soil; extraction of minerals; transport; trade; public forces; administration; arts and professions; domestic services; subsistence on pension, interest and rent; labour of all sorts; and finally beggary and prostitution: *Census Punjab 1911,* Pt II, 427-35. The occupational categories remain the same in the census reports of 1921 and 1931.

[5] Settlement reports of Gurdaspur, Amritsar, Lahore, Montgomery, Panipat and Karnal, Shahpur, Ludhiana and Gurdaspur are particularly useful.

[6] Gazetteers of the districts of Amritsar, Ferozepur, Gujrat, Gujranwala, Gurdaspur, Jalandhar, Jhang, Ludhiana, Montgomery, Multan, Shahpur, Sialkot and the Chenab Colony (1904) contain useful information on the *sepi* system.

in the gazetteers, it is possible to get a fair picture of the economic condition of the artisans in the traditional set-up.

Monographs on different 'industries', such as iron and steel, cotton, woollen, gold and silver, brass and copper, wood and leather were published between 1884 and 1907 by the government of Punjab.[7] These monographs deal mainly with implements and the methods of work and the overall state and prospects of the manufacturing activity in the countryside and in urban areas. They also notice, although briefly, the castes engaged in production and the wages and profits earned by them. In spite of their brevity, these monographs provide some useful information on the village artisans and their changing socio-economic relationships in the traditional set-up and thus supplement the data from the census and other reports.[8]

Economic surveys of fifteen villages in the Punjab conducted during the 1930s refer to the artisans both as traditional servants of village societies and as independently engaged skilled workers. These village surveys also throw some light on the physical and occupational mobility among the artisans.[9]

Stray information on artisans can be culled from various other reports, like those on internal trade and manufactures, on prices and wages or those of the Indian Industrial Commission and Famine Commissions. Some pamphlets such as on poorer artisans of Lahore published by the Board of Economic Inquiry, Punjab and the decennial reports on the Material and Moral Progress of Punjab contain useful information on the condition of various artisan groups in the province.

[7] Forbes Watson in 1872 had initiated the idea to prepare monographs on various industries: *Progs. Commerce and Industry,* July 1908.

[8] Some more monographs were compiled during the 1920s and the 1930s under the auspices of the Board of Economic Inquiry, Punjab. They deal primarily with the economic condition of the 'industries' covered by them.

[9] Village surveys of Gaggar-Bhana, Suner, Durrana-Langna are particularly helpful.

III

Notwithstanding their usefulness, our sources suffer from some serious limitations. Most of the difficulties in working with these sources spring from the basic drawback that the concept of actual workers or the criteria according to which entries were made are not clearly defined.[10] Discrepancy in numbers between the persons returned as belonging to a particular caste and those returned as following the profession by which the caste was known is the first problem that arises from this lack of definition. The 1881 census returns, for example, show 5,08,008 persons as belonging to the Tarkhan caste, whereas the number of carpenters is only 1,66,536—32 per cent of the former. Similarly the number of those belonging to the Lohar caste is given at 2,64,720 and those returned actually engaged as blacksmiths number only 59,502 or 22.48 per cent of the Lohar caste. Julahas are listed at 5,52,944 and the number of weavers given is 3,87,633 or 70 per cent of the Julahas. There are similar discrepancies in case of the Sunars, Kumhars and the Mochis.[11]

On the other hand, according to the census returns of 1891, the number of persons engaged in some professions is more than those actually belonging to the corresponding castes. For instance, the returns for the Julaha caste are 5,94,995, but the number of weavers given is 9,21,501. There is no indication of the identity of those returned as weavers but not belonging to the caste. Nor can it be said with any certainty that all the Julahas were weavers, as there must have been some minors, children and aged people who could not be returned as actually working. Similarly, the number of calico-dyers is

[10] The difficulty in identifying the workers or making distinctions between the bread winners and dependents has been brought out also in a study on labour force in Tamilnadu: Newell, 179-81; also Sharma (1978), 147-51.

[11] For detail, see *Census Punjab 1881*, Vol. II, Table XI A-B. The number of the Sunars was 1,35,345 and the goldsmiths were 50,864; the number of the Kumhars was 1,22,586, whereas the potters numbered 90,909; the Mochis numbered, 3,22,873 and the shoe-makers, 1,67,087. The difficulty in reconciling the data remains in the later census reports as well.

given at 27,975, whereas that of the Lilari caste is 25,010.[12] Therefore, it is difficult to establish that all those returned as engaged in a particular occupation belonged to the corresponding caste as well. The early census reports do not provide satisfactory clue to those who belonged to a caste but did not pursue its traditional occupation. In fact, they have not been identified in these reports. Their proportions, therefore, can not be established with any precision. These reports do not even account for the movement of the people of the artisan castes from one occupation to another. On the whole, with varying concepts and definitions the data of 1881 and 1891 censuses are not comparable. In 1881, for instance, 59,502 blacksmiths were enumerated in the Punjab, but in 1891 their number was put at 1,51,779. In case of the goldsmiths their number in 1881 was 38,723 and in 1891 it was 1,67,081.

However, from 1901 onwards, the censuses started paying attention to occupational mobility and even tried to clarify the concept of entries with reference to their economic import.[13] In the census reports of 1901, 1911 and 1921, all persons who actually did the work and did not live on rents and pensions were deemed to be 'actual workers'. These reports considered each individual either as an 'actual worker' or a 'dependent'. In addition to the working men, only those women and children were shown as workers who added to the family income by working regularly and not occasionally. But the definition for the working age was not explicit. A boy, for instance, who looked after his father's cattle occasionally was considered as a 'dependent', but the one who did so regularly was an 'actual worker'. The census of 1931 introduced a new concept for recording those engaged in an 'economic' activity by distinguishing 'earners' from 'working dependents'and the latter from 'dependents'. The 'earners' were those who worked personally or with the help of servants. The

[12] *Census Punjab 1891*, pt II, 273-95 and 420-27.

[13] For a detailed discussion on the concept of entries in Indian censuses from 1901 to 1961, see Krishnamurthy, 323-37.

'working dependents' were those who worked to augment family income but did not work to earn separate wages.

Furthermore, information from two government sources, of the same period is not necessarily identical. According to the census report of 1868, for instance, there were 1,57,917 blacksmiths in the Punjab, but according to the revenue administration report of 1869-70 there were only 23,507 'workers in iron'. Similarly, according to the census report of 1868, there were 51,395 'weavers' in Jalandhar district, while the revenue administration report of 1869-70 gives the number of 'weavers' at 1,042 only.[14] To cite another case, the number of 'weavers' in Panipat and Karnal parganas according to the settlement report of 1872-80 was 1,825, whereas according to the census report of 1881, in the whole of Karnal district, comprising the tahsils of Panipat, Kaithal and Karnal there were 7,929 'weavers'.[15] How do we account for such differences?

We do not have any explanation for the fluctuations or discrepancies in the number of people engaged in various occupations between 1868 and 1891. The differences between the census returns of 1868 and 1891 are marginal and seem to be comparable. For example, in 1868, the blacksmiths numbered 1,57,917 and in 1891 their number is given at 1,51,779. However, the figures for blacksmiths in the census report of 1881 are much smaller than those of the preceding and succeeding reports, to the extent of 62.32 per cent less than 1868 figures and 137.72 per cent less than the 1891 returns. Similarly inexplicable discrepancies as table I shows have been found in case of the figures for carpenters, potters, shoe-makers, goldsmiths and weavers.

Non-comparability of the data is a serious difficulty that we face while using the census returns. 'Even were it possible to reconcile all definitional differences between the censuses', it is almost impossible to compare the data provided in one

[14] See for detail, *Census Punjab 1868,* Table IV and *Revenue Administration Report 1869-70*, Table xxxvii.

[15] *See SR Panipat and Karnal 1872-80*, 116; *Census Punjab 1881,* pt II, Table XII, A-B.

TABLE I: DIFFERENCES BETWEEN THE DATA AVAILABLE FROM CENSUSES OF 1868, 1881 AND 1891.

Occupation	*1868*	*1881*	*1891*	*Percentage difference between*		
				1868 and 1881	*1881 and 1891*	*1868 and 1891*
Blacksmiths	1,57,917	59,502	1,51,779	–62.32	+137.71	–3.89
Carpenters	2,46,409	1,06,536	2,43,441	–56.76	+166.05	+15.03
Potters	2,02,609	81,565	2,22,896	–57.30	+236.76	+10.01
Shoe-makers	2,98,220	1,56,396	5,26,267	–47.56	+236.76	+76.47
Goldsmiths	1,17,726	38,723	1,67,081	–67.11	+331.76	+41.92
Weavers	9,24,158	3,87,633	9,21,501	–58.06	+137.71	–0.28

Adapted from: *Census Punjab 1868*, Table IV, *Census Punjab 1881,* Pt II, Table XIII-A, *Census Punjab 1891*, Pt II.

census report with that given in another.[16] The difficulty arises particularly when we look at the table entitled 'Occupations of Castes and Tribes' in the reports of years 1911, 1921 and 1931. The census of 1911 contains data relevant for the whole of the Punjab, but in the reports of 1921 and 1931, the artisans are subsumed under different communities and the data are given region-wise for the central, western and the eastern plains in the Punjab and the Punjab Hills. The same difficulty is experienced in case of other tables, like those on the literacy among the artisans.[17]

Kingslay Davis exonerates the census officials for the drawbacks in the data on the ground that the 'census officials were scholars and government men first and statisticians afterwards'.[18] The discrepancies in figures and the lack of uniform criteria for classification notwithstanding, the variety of information provided by the census and other official reports on the artisans is invaluable. On the basis of this information, supplemented by non-government sources, field work and oral evidence, it has been possible to identify the trends and arrive at some broad generalizations about the changing social relationships consequent upon the changes in the socio-economic condition of the artisans in the Punjab under colonial rule.

[16] Newell, 181.

[17] The census of 1891 gives the most detailed information on literacy among the artisan castes: *Census Punjab 1891*, Pt II, 630-97. Information from later censuses is partial.

[18] Davis observes further that Indian censuses are remarkable not only for the information they reveal but also for the special obstacle they had to overcome, that is, the vastness of the country and suspicions of the people about any innovations: 4-5.

CHAPTER TWO

Traditional Socio-Economic Set-up

The society in the Punjab did not entirely conform to the traditional hierarchical pattern.[1] Every community had grades of position and distinctions of rank governed by the considerations of descent and calling.[2] Social status was based on the evaluation of a caste or an occupational group in terms of 'high' and 'low' which broadly corresponded to control over resources and skills and the economic benefits ensuing from it.[3] This was particularly true of the agrarian social structure in the Punjab which was fundamentally a labour structure, composed of interrelated specialized services performed by distinct castes.[4] The persons working in an occupation generally belonged to the same caste which made the division of labour in the countryside relatively ascriptive and the economic system to a certain extent non-competitive.[5] In this situation the general attitudes towards the menials and outcastes who constituted nearly one-fifth of the total

[1] The land-holding Jats and Rajputs in rural areas and the trading Khatris in urban areas claimed the status of the *kshtriya*. The Banias had the *vaisya* status in the *varna* system. But the Brahmans did not enjoy the favoured position assigned to them by tradition or enjoyed by the Brahmans elsewhere in the country: Srinivas, 4-10; Dungen (1968), 54-98; and Grewal (1981).

[2] Ibbetson, 3.

[3] Social status here implies the perceived relationship of a person, a social group, or a category of persons to others: Laswell, 143.

[4] In the Punjab specialization of interrelated services can not be perceived as 'traditionalized in religious matrix' as Cox understood it: 67.

[5] This is particularly true of the occupations evaluated as socially 'low': K.N. Sharma, 30.

population in the Punjab,[6] were perhaps relatively more tolerant.[7] The artisans in the Punjab were, nevertheless, universally considered socially low. Among them the Sunars, Tarkhans, Lohars, Kumhars and the Julahas were regarded as 'clean'and the Chamars and Mochis as 'unclean' artisans.[8] Whether Muslim, Hindu or Sikh, the 'clean' artisan castes were broadly treated at par with the *sudra* of Hindu *varna* system.[9] On account of relatively 'clean' nature of their work, the castes of goldsmiths, carpenters, blacksmiths and potters were considered superior among the artisans. The weavers were regarded as lowest among the 'clean' castes.[10] Chamars and Mochis who worked in leather were considered the lowest, in fact, untouchables.[11]

However, the Chamars constituted the single largest social group among the artisans, constituting 24 per cent of their total population. They were followed by the Julaha, Kumhar, Lohar, Mochi, Sunar, and the Tarkhan castes. The other castes, such as the Kalal (wine- distillers), Lilari (calico-dyers), Raj (Masons) and the Penja (cotton-carders) were much smaller in number.[12] Considering the requirements of the agrarian society, it may be reasonable to assume that the proportion of artisans living in rural areas was much higher than those living in urban areas.

II

The artisans served the village society with their specialized skills. They manufactured the articles of wood, metal, leather and clay. They also produced cloth, sugar and oil for local

[6] *Census Punjab 1881*, pt II, Table VIII-A.

[7] Douie (1916), 106.

[8] Ibbetson, 267; see also Bhattacharya, 179-215.

[9] Ibbetson, 268; Douie (1916), 32-33; Dungen, 68.

[10] Ibbetson, 302-03.

[11] In western parts of the Punjab the Muslim workers in leather were called Mochis and in eastern and central districts they were called the Chamars: Ibbetson, 297.

[12] See chapter three below.

needs. They were involved in practically all work requiring their labour and professional skills, like sowing, reaping, oil-milling, grinding of grain, pressing of sugarcane and the preparation of *gur* including manufacturing of sugarcane press and boiling pans. In short, the artisans were indispensable for agricultural operations.

The artisans worked for the village land-owners under the *sepi* arrangements known also as the *jajmani* system.[13] This system of interdependence in which each caste in a village performed a form of service for the others involved mutual obligations for work and payment. It signified relationship between food producing families and those who provided services and goods and were collectively labelled as *kamins*.[14] This system ensured regularity in the labour supply for the dominant agricultural castes and livelihood for the *kamins*.[15] Each family of artisans was attached to certain agriculturist families to whom they served and furnished certain amount of goods and services according to their particular occupational calling. Under these arrangements the artisans were called *sepis* or the *sepidars*. They had fixed duties and remuneration. For extra work, if called upon to do any, they were paid for separately. An important characteristic of this system at the opening of our period was that it operated without much exchange of cash.[16]

The artisan family's right to their clients was treated as a sort of property right.[17] Even if a client or clients were dissatisfied with their *kamins*, it was difficult to find a substitute because none from the same caste would work as a replacement and even if one volunteered to do so he was ostracized from the caste. The members of each caste and

[13] The term *jajman* originally referred to the client for whom the Brahman priest performed rituals. It is now generally used to refer to the patron or the recipient of specialized services: Wiser, xxii.

[14] The *kamins* are known by different terms in other parts in India such as *paryan*, *pradhan*, and *balutedar*: Mandelbaum, 164.

[15] Lewis, 57.

[16] Lewis, 59; Eglar, 2.

[17] Mandelbaum, 167-68.

occupation cooperated among themselves to maintain adequate service level for all patrons. In a situation in which a Lohar or Tarkhan was unable to work for the clients a substitute was provided by the *biradri* who performed services in addition to his own and without any compensation either from the caste fellow or the land-owner.[18] The rights and advantages were thus secured by tradition.

The most important among the *sepidars* were those whose assistance in agricultural operations was vital like the carpenters (Tarkhans), potters (Kumhars), blacksmiths (Lohars), and the leather-workers (Chamars and Mochis). The Tarkhans and Kumhars were called as *vade kamins* or superiors while the Lohars and the Mochis were the *laude* or inferior *Kamins*.[19]

The carpenters with the raw materials supplied by the *jajman* were required to make and repair all wooden agricultural implements and articles for domestic use. They manufactured and repaired ploughs and furnished handles to sickles and spades once in a year, besides one pitch-fork. They manufactured also the household furniture and articles for day to day use which consisted mostly of the cots (*charpai*) and low square stool (*pirhi*) and the spinning wheel (*charkha*).[20]

The blacksmiths furnished and repaired iron implements like the *datri, hal, kahi, kohara, khurpa, karhaha* for boiling sugar-cane juice, and several other metal wares used by agriculturists.[21] The cost of the raw materials for new implements was borne by the owners, but the blacksmiths had to furnish iron for repair work.[22]

[18] Lewis, 58.

[19] *SR Montgomery 1892-99*, 29. The literal meaning of *laude* is young or small.

[20] For the obligations of the Tarkhans see *SR Montgomery 1878*, 29, 80; *SR Jalandhar 1880-86*, 87; *SR Ludhiana 1878-83*, 140; *SR Lahore 1865-69*, 61-62; *DG Sialkot*, 57-58; *DG Gujrat*, 63.

[21] English equivalents are given in the glossary.

[22] For the functions of the Lohars see *SR Montgomery 1878*, 80; *SR Lahore 1865-69*, 62; *DG Sialkot*, 57; *DG Gujrat*, 63.

The potters supplied earthen pots, called *tind*, used for drawing water from wells for irrigation purposes. These vessels were tied round the persian wheel in a row. A well for irrigation purposes required about one thousand to two thousand *tinds* in a year and a Kumhar family could serve only three to four wells. As regards the supply of earthen vessels for domestic use, one family of Kumhar usually met the requirements of fourteen or fifteen houses and supplied about twenty large and twenty-five small vessels per house. These included the vessels to store water and to cook food: the *gharha, surahi, karhni and tourhi,* or the *handi* were the important items. The potters also helped in carrying the agricultural produce to the market on their donkeys.[23]

The leather-workers or the Chamars and Mochis supplied shoes, leather-thongs, blinders for bullocks, and harnesses and whips. For making these articles they removed, dressed and dyed the hides and skins of the dead cattle. They had, however, no right over the hides of animals killed for food. When not engaged in their traditional profession they were required to do several other tasks like white-washing the guest house of the village, or plastering of the houses of the *jajmans* with mud.[24]

The 'specialization' of the village artisans under the *sepi* system did not involve fine work which was beyond their skills, particularly because of their immobility and the relative lack of contact with the outside world. Moreover, the local requirements did not demand much refinement in manufactures. The village Lohar, for example, was mainly concerned with turning out ordinary articles such as plough-shares, axes and pots and pans. These articles, were 'crude but fairly strong' which was enough to serve the local needs. The

[23] The position of Kumhars as *sepidars* was recognized in every district except Kangra: *Monograph* on *Pottery*, 27. Kessinger, however, does not include potter among the *sepidars* in the village studied by him: 62. See also *SR Lahore 1865-69*, 61-62; *DG Sialkot*, 57-58; *SR Ludhiana 1878-83*, 52.

[24] For duties of the Chamars and the Mochis, see *SR Montgomery 1878*, 29, 80; *SR Panipat and Karnal 1872-80*, 116; *Census Punjab 1881*, pt I, 384; *DG Gurgaon*, 65; *DG Jalandhar*, 87; *DG Sialkot*, 57-58.

method of manufacturing was also of the same order. The Lohar simply hammered out a piece of iron into the desired shape, working cold if possible and heating it only when necessary. The furnace was generally made of mud, and charcoal was used as fuel.[25] The work of the village Tarkhan too was not much refined because of the limited requirements of the agriculturists. Even the well-to-do people in villages did not require more than a few cots (*charpais*) and stools (*pirhis*), besides some metal utensils and earthen-wares.[26]

The remuneration of the *sepidars* varied from place to place and was determined by local customs. They were paid in kind by a fixed share of the produce from land. The dues of the artisans under the *sep* system were deducted from the produce of the village before making any other payment. The deduction generally allowed was 10 to 16 per cent of the total produce. In Jalandhar, for example, it amounted to 16 per cent; in Batala in Gurdaspur district it was about 12 per cent, and in Amritsar the deduction allowed was between 13 and 15 per cent of the total produce.[27]

Generally, the remuneration of blacksmiths, carpenters, and the potters was at almost the same rates. In Sialkot they received at each harvest one sheaf (*bhari*) of corn weighing about a maund and six seers of grain at the rate of per plough per household. They were entitled to have the last pickings of cotton. In addition, the blacksmiths received two *tinds* or *chattis* (earthen pitcher) of sugarcane juice daily when employed for making the boiling pan and a ball of *gur* weighing about two seers during the period the sugarcane

[25] *Monograph on Iron and Steel*, 1, 92.

[26] Referring to the bareness of the houses in villages and the simplicity of their construction, Vera Anstey remarks that 'Indian dwellings in rural areas deserve the title of huts rather than of houses':30.

[27] *AR Amritsar 1913*, 28; Douie(1899), 90. In 1878, a cultivator in the village Palasaur in Amritsar district with a total income of rupees 1418 and 6 annas expended rupees 181 and 3 annas on the remuneration of artisans and menials which works out to be 13 per cent of the total: *Punjab Report in Reply to Inquiries Issued by the Famine Commission 1878-79*, Vol. I, 444-45.

press was in operation. They also received a bundle from each crop for furnishing a *datri* (reaping hook).[28] The carpenter too was entitled to special fees. He was paid from one rupee and four annas to two rupees for making the sugarcane press (*velna*) and keeping it in order. He was entitled to one seer of *gur* daily while the mill was in operation.[29] At some places, he was paid five rupees in cash and ten *marlas* of fodder for furnishing a *bair* (wooden wheel of the well).[30] The cultivators were supposed to provide meals during the days the carpenter was at work. The carpenters also made well-pulleys and the upright bodies of the ploughs (*munna*) for which they were entitled to special fees.[31]

The Chamars and Mochis, however, were paid at half the rates of the Tarkhans, Lohars and the Kumhars. Their dues also varied from place to place. In Jalandhar the leather-workers were entitled to receive one-fourth seer out of every maund of the produce. In Hoshiarpur, the rate was one seer per maund or one-fortieth of the produce. In Sialkot, they were entitled to cut crop on a small portion of land or two or three sheaves of grain and some grain on the threshing floor. In Gujrat, the leather-workers got two sheaves per plough and one *pai* or eight seers of grain or one sheaf of corn and a *dropa* or about three seers of grain lying on the threshing floor from each household.[32]

On social ceremonies, like marriages and births, the *sepidars*, particularly the Lohars, Tarkhans and Kumhars, made ritual accessories such as the bridal seats and tables for worship, and vessels for dowry for their patrons. For these

[28] A bundle was equivalent of one-third of a sheaf or *bhari*.

[29] *AR Tarn Taran 1912*, 28; *DG Sialkot*, 57-58; *DG Montgomery*, 80; *SR Jalandhar 1880-87*, 86.

[30] *Marla* is a measure of land containing 30 $^{1}/_{2}$ square yards. *Bair* means the wheel on which well pots are strung and revolve. It is made of 28 spokes (*tir*), 28 tires (*Vanang*) and 19 cross pieces connecting the outer and the inner tires on which the well rope and pots (*tinds*) rest.

[31] For detail on payments to carpenters see *An Economic Survey of Durrana-Langna*, 32-33.

[32] *Monograph on Leather Industry*, 5.

services they were entitled to a fee known as the *lag* and were called *lagis*.[33] The services of the other artisans were required from time to time because of the periodic festivals and the prevalence of the dowry system. The materials used were ordinarily provided by the customers. The requirements of cloth and ornaments were furnished by the weavers and the goldsmiths. The articles thus manufactured were not covered under the *sep* system, and the artisans were paid according to the specific services.[34]

In the sowing and reaping operations the artisans, were employed to do work in fields. They were paid separately for serving in their non-professional capacity for weeding, reaping, threshing, sifting and stacking of the crop. In Shahpur district for instance, they were paid two rupees per acre for reaping, one sheaf out of twentyone for threshing, and four seers of corn per day for cleaning.[35]

On other occasions, and for miscellaneous purposes, the Chamars were expected to render unpaid labour or *begar* and were called *begaris*.[36] The *begar* included carrying the fodder for cattle of the land-owners from the fields, white-washing the village guest-house; carrying the luggage of the visiting officials from one place to another, and attending to their comforts during their stay in the village.[37] For these services they were given small tips.

The village artisans were subjected to a cess, on hearths realized by proprietors from other residents in the village.[38]

[33] *A lagi* generally is a menial or a functionary at marriages entitled to fixed fees: *The Punjabi Dictionary*, 650.

In *Vilyatpur* too practice of paying to artisans and menials on special occasions was in existence but Kessinger does not use the term *lagi* for them: 68. Mandelbaum refers to these payments to *kamins* as small tips for a score of special services rendered by them: 168. See also, Eglar, 200.

[34] The position of weavers and goldsmiths remained broadly the same in other parts of India too: see for example, Madelbaum, 162; also Kulkarni, 157-62.

[35] *DG Shahpur*, 39.

[36] *Census Punjab 1881*, pt I, 384.

[37] *SR Panipat and Karnal 1872-79*, 115-16.

[38] Douie (1899), 48.

Called *kudhi-kamini* in eastern Punjab, it was known as *haq-buha* or door cess in western districts. It has also been called *ahtiraf* or *muhtarifa*, paid by the artisans to the proprietors of the village in which they plied their trade or *hirfa*.[39] In Lahore, it was called *chak-atrafi* and *dharat*.[40] In Amritsar this cess was known simply as *kamini*.[41] It was known also as *chulha* tax. At places across the Satlej, it was collected simply as *sair-dehi* (village-cess) or as *Chowkidara* or watchman's salary.[42] However, *kudhi-kamini* remained the most commonly used term for this cess.

The rate of collection of *kudhi-kamini* in the Punjab generally was two rupees per annum, payable half yearly by each adult male engaged in his calling.[43] This cess was a part of the income of the state in the early nineteenth century. Under the British, however, the land-owners were allowed to collect it for the *malba* or the common fund of the village.[44] After spending the amount from the collection of *kudhi-kamini* on the watchman's salary the rest was credited to the *malba*.[45]

The object of *kudhi-kamini* was perhaps to transfer a share of the burden of hospitality and maintenance of the village on

---

H.H. Wilson translates *kudhi* as a family hearth or a place or stone where food is cooked. The term is derived from the Sanskrit term *kuti* meaning a house or a village or inhabitant or a tenant: 37. Ibbetson spells the tax as *kurhi-kamini: SR Panipat and Karnal 1872-80*, 108.

[39] Douie (1899), 40. *Ahtiraf* spelled also as *ihtiraf* means the one skilful in any art or trade; *muhtarifa* is a Persian word for tax on trades and professions; *sair-dehi* means a village cess, and *hirfa* is a trade, craft, art, business or profession: Steingass, 20, 416, 1183.

[40] *SR Lahore 1865-69*, 36.

[41] *SR Amritsar 1860*, 56.

[42] *Foreign Political Proceedings, 31 December 1847*, No. 25; *DG Gurgaon*, 52.

[43] *SR Shahpur 1887-94*, 52. See also Sharma (1980), 177-86.

[44] At some places, *kudhi-kamini* was counted as a source of income of the state by the early British administrators as well. In Sampla tahsil of Rohtak district, for instance, 8,388 rupees were collected as *kudhi-kamini* in 1876. In Jhajhar tahsil about 5,600 rupees were assessed as income from *kudhi-kamini* in 1868: *AR Sampla 1876*, np; *AR Jhajhar 1868*, Table XV.

[45] Douie (1899), 42.

to the non-agriculturists as well.[46] Those who abandoned their traditional calling and adopted agriculture as their occupation were exempted from its payment. At times, the artisans tried to evade the payment of *kudhi-kamini* and the Julahas at Shahpur were even reported to have protested against its collection.[47]

The *sepi* system or the traditional relationship managed to ensure the poverty and low social standing of the artisans.[48] The land-owners maintained their economic power and social superiority by obliging the artisans to subsist on the professional and non-professional services. The artisans were the first victims of any failure in crops owing to their being extremely poor and living a hand to mouth existence. Famines, floods, droughts and epidemics hit them the hardest as they did not have the means to tide over difficult phases.[49] The chances of an average artisan to supplement his income by working outside the *sep* system too were rather limited.

The artisans, in fact, had to face all sorts of hardships and humiliation. They could be beaten over trivial issues; and they were not allowed to share the same platform on social and religious gatherings. The artisans could not enter even the shrines of *pirs* and *babas* on particular festivals let alone other religious establishments because the dominant agriculturist castes would not allow that.[50] In larger villages the artisans of

[46] *SR Panipat and Karnal 1872-80*, 108-9. The scavengers (Chuhras) and the barbers (Nais) were exempted from the payment of this cess: *Progs. Foreign/Political Department, December 1867*, No. 1832.

[47] *SR Shahpur 1887-94*, 52.

[48] The spirit of caste among other things includes an element of mutual repulsion, which means that different groups in the society repel one another and that each retires within itself and isolates itself: Bougle, 9. The element of repulsion existed also in the land-owner—artisan relationship. Because of their economic dependence on the land-owners the artisans in general and the lower evaluated artisans in particular, however, could not adopt openly such an attitude towards the land-owners. See also Cox, 5,70.

[49] *Famine Commission Report 1878-79*, Vol III, 10, 11, 358.

[50] The available evidence suggest that in towns and cities also, the lower evaluated castes like the Chamars, Julahas, Lohars and the Tarkhans, and other artisan castes experienced discrimination in religious places: see

different castes were expected to live within their separate residential enclosures or *galis*. The Chamars, however, were supposed to live away from the main residential site.[51] The situation was not much different in urban areas.

III

The artisans in towns and cities were apparently free from some of the constraints felt by their counterparts in rural areas. The urban artisans were broadly of two descriptions. One, the specialists who manufactured goods and articles in their specialized trade according to the requirements of their clients. They used their own implements and raw material and were paid by the job. The others worked in shops and factories on daily wage basis or on contract.[52] The implements and raw materials were provided to them by their employers.

The products of the urban artisans were more varied and generally more sophisticated.[53] They produced textile fabrics, jewellery, knives, razors, iron-chests, safes, almirahs, iron buckets, nails, locks, earthen-wares, toys and several other articles of daily use in urban areas. Important manufacturing centres were at Amritsar, Lahore, Sialkot, Gujrat, Jhang, Hoshiarpur, Jalandhar and Multan. Amritsar was known for silks, shawls, wood carving, ornaments of gold and silver. Multan and Lahore were known for their silks also. The weavers of Jalandhar, Hoshiarpur and Sialkot were known for their fine *susi* cloth and varieties of *lachas* and *lungis*. Jhang was known for coarse cotton cloth.[54]

The earnings of skilled workers in urban areas ranged between 5 and 15 rupees per month. Among them were also

---

Jones (1974), 130-35.

51 See also Kessinger, 60.

52 Trevaskis, 270.

53 The technical skills and abilities of urban carpenters prompted Baden-Powell to comment on their work that it was 'careful in execution and to the minutest detail': 272, 282.

54 *Punjab Administration Report 1869-70*, 110; Monograph on Iron and Steel, 2; Badenoch, 5; Baden-Powell, 272; *Census Punjab 1881*, pt I, 385.

the carpenters and blacksmiths employed in the construction of bridges, drains (*nallas*) and canals.[55] The rates of wages for the unskilled artisans were much less. Those who worked under the 'capitalist traders' around 1900 earned 3 annas to 5 annas a day. For women and children the wages were even lesser. They could get 2 annas to 4 annas a day.[56] This income was barely enough for their subsistence and with no opportunity in a nearly stagnant economic situation. The arrangement of advances by the employer or trader to operatives virtually rendered them as 'bonded' labour.[57] The advance or the debt was called *baqi*. The debt generally ranged from 300 rupees to 1000 rupees. This amount was never deducted from the wages and remained outstanding against their names.[58] Under this arrangement the artisans could not leave the employer without clearing the dues outstanding against their names, which they were seldom able to do.[59] The urban artisans thus mostly remained on the wrong side of the ledger. The economic condition of the artisans in towns on the whole was not substantially better than their counterparts in villages. They had to be content with the wages ranging between 2 and 7 annas a day. The rural artisans could feel more secure in the knowledge of their

[55] *Proceedings Foreign Department, September 1850*, 77-81; *Annual Report on the Working of Indian Factory Act of 1907 for the year 1907 in the Punjab*, 1-18; *ibid., 1909*,1-33; *ibid., 1914*, 1-23, *ibid., 1915*, 1.

[56] *Imperial Gazetteer of India*, Vol. XX, 320.

[57] See Sharma (1983), 507-08.

[58] *Census Punjab 1901*, pt I, 368-71.

[59] In fact, the chain of exploitation was indirectly accentuated also by the government. Earlier, till the 1850s, the custom was as follows: when an artisan left one employer to join the other without repaying the advance in any form, his debts were also transferred to the second employer who was held responsible for their repayment. Under this practice it was possible for the artisans to move from one employer to another. In 1858, the government through a circular ordered that the second employer could not be held responsible for the debts of their artisans and that only the artisans themselves were responsible for their debts: '*Circular issued by the Judicial Commissoner of the Punjab to Commissioners and Superintendents of the Punjab 29th October 1858*, No. 192.

indispensability to rural economy and of the certainty of their remuneration under *sepi* arrangements.[60]

IV

The traditional set up guaranteed the artisans a living. The artisans understood that their low economic level and social status was due to the nature of their work, they continued to work in it, also because the dominant sections controlling interests in both rural and urban areas would not easily allow them to move outside the existing system.[61] At the same time, the *biradri* of hereditary artisans discouraged them from entering into any new trade. Those who dared were the object of ridicule in the *biradari* and could even be ostracized.[62] Moreover, at the outset of our period, with much limited diversification of economic activity, there had been very few openings for the skilled artisans outside the traditional relationship. Their scope in domestic jobs in urban areas or in the service of the state too appears to have been limited because of the considerations of caste.

Due to the rapidly changing socio-economic environment in the British Punjab the framework of traditional relationship

[60] *Famine Commission Report 1878-79*, Vol. III, 19; *Census Punjab 1881*, pt I, 384.

[61] In Vilyatpur in 1896, a weaver who wished to migrate from the village had to face resistance from the local proprietary group: Kessinger, 60.

[62] P.S. Sodhbans interviewed some Tarkhans of Lahore in 1941 who stated that their family traditions were such that they could not give up carpentry for fear of action against them:8.

A respondent interviewed by the author explained that he opened a *pan* (betel-leaf) shop after leaving carpentry, but was not allowed to continue for more than six months by his brothers and kinsmen and he felt obliged to come back to carpentry. Another respondent confided that no caste would allow any outsider to join its occupation for fear of leaking out the secrets of trade. So much so that even within the families, secrecy was strictly maintained. The weavers, for example, would not tell the secrets of their trade to their daughters so that they may not pass these on to their husband's family. But the daughter-in-law was generally told of the trade secrets.

between the artisans and land-owners was significantly altered. A considerable proportion of the artisans moved out of the village, and in many cases, altogether changed their occupations. These circumstances had a bearing on their demographic distribution as well.

CHAPTER THREE

Demographic Distribution

Demographic distribution of the artisan castes was related fairly closely to the general demographic set up in the Punjab. More than 85 per cent of the people of the province lived in villages.[1] The majority of population was concentrated in the fertile and agriculturally well developed central districts of the plains. These districts covered about one-fourth of the area of the Punjab and contained more than 50 per cent of its population.[2]

The artisan castes, particularly the Chamar, Julaha, Kumhar, Lohar, Mochi, Tarkhan and the Sunar, constituted nearly 18 per cent of the total population of the province.[3] They were concentrated in the countryside of the central districts, because in this area the general standard of agriculture was comparatively high and so was the dependence of cultivators

[1] The ratio between urban and rural population remained about the same throughout the period. The percentage of the population living in the countryside in the Punjab was : 86.14 in 1881; 89 in 1911 and 87 in 1931: *Census Punjab 1881*, pt II, Table I; *Census Punjab 1911*, pt II, 2; *Census Punjab 1931*, pt II, Table I.

[2] The central districts of the Punjab plains included Hoshiarpur, Jalandhar, Ludhiana, Ferozepur, Lahore, Amritsar, Gurdaspur, Sialkot, Gujranwala, Sheikhupura, Gujrat, Lyallpur, and Jhang.

The percentage of the total population in these districts was: 50.23 in 1881; 51.21 in 1891; 52.55 in 1901; 51.32 in 1911; 52.15 in 1921 and 52.68 in 1931: *Census Punjab 1921*, pt II, np; *Census Punjab 1931*, pt II, 3.

[3] In 1881, the population of the artisan castes in the central districts was 14,89,187 out of the total population of 85,09,138: *Census Punjab 1881*, pt II, 1-4.

on the artisans.[4] A well-cultivated populous hinterland also accounted for the existence of a large number of towns and the two cities of Amritsar and Lahore. In the upper portions of the Bari Doab alone the number of urban centres was around 25 at the outset of the British rule. These included, besides Amritsar and Lahore, Bahrampur, Batala, Dera Baba Nanak, Dinanagar, Jandiala, Khem Karan, Pathankot, Patti, Qadian, Sri Hargobindpur and Tarn Taran.[5] Apart from offering opportunities for employment, the nearby urban centres could provide additional markets for the products of the more skilled among the artisans.[6]

II

A comparison of the figures for the artisan castes with the general population figures suggests a broad conformity between the two. The population of the Punjab was more than 85 lacs in 1881 and the artisan castes were enumerated at nearly 15 lacs, forming over 17 per cent of the total. The total population increased to 95 lacs in 1891, at an annual rate of 1.22 per cent or 12.24 per cent for the decade. The annual rate of increase among the artisans during the decade 1881-1891 was 1.44 per cent and their total was over 17 lacs. Besides the absence of any major natural calamity during the period this general increase has been attributed to the extension in the total area under cultivation and enhanced agricultural production.[7]

In 1901, the total population of the Punjab was recorded at 104 lacs. The population increased at an annual rate of .69 per cent during 1891-1901.[8] The number of the artisan castes also rose to about 18 lacs showing an increase of 10.22 per

[4] In western districts 'labour was not so often procured from beyond the limits of cultivator's family': *Census Punjab 1881*, pt I, 384.

[5] Reeta Grewal, Appendix I. See also Banga (1981), 200-01.

[6] Sharma (1983), 506-07.

[7] *Census Punjab 1891*, pt II, 10-11; *Census Punjab 1931*, pt I, 15-16.

[8] Calculations are based on the data given in *Census Punjab 1921*, pt I, 2; Mitra, Vol I, 14.

cent for the decade, at the rate of 1.02 per cent per annum. This decline in the overall rate of growth over the previous decade was due mainly to the spread of cholera in 1892, the plague in 1897-98 and of famine in 1898-99 which raised the death rate in the Punjab.[9]

The decade between 1901-1911 was marked by decrease in the total population figures from 104 to 100 lacs, declining at an annual rate of .40 per cent or by -4.07 per cent for the decade.[10] The figures for the artisan castes also came down to 17.5 lacs, at an annual rate of -.68 per cent and the decennial rate of -6.78 per cent.[11] This decrease was due again to the recurring influenza, the plague and the fever. Four and a half million deaths from the fever were recorded in the province during this period. The plague of 1907-08 alone was responsible for two million deaths.[12] The effects of these epidemics were more marked in the densely populated districts of Amritsar, Gurdaspur, Jalandhar and Sialkot.[13]

By 1921, however, there was a noticeable change and the total population rose to more than 107 lacs, growing at the rate of .73 per cent per annum or 7.3 per cent during the decade. During this period the population of the artisan castes also rose slightly to 17.8 lacs, indicating an average rate of increase of .19 per cent per annum or 1.93 per cent for the decade. This increase was despite the influenza of 1918 which accounted for the death of about a million people in the Punjab.[14]

The period between 1921 and 1931 was relatively normal and the total population increased to 124 lacs, showing an

[9] *Census Punjab 1931*, pt I, 16-17.

Trevaskis, however, maintains that after 1880 scarcity was a local problem and could be relieved by moving grain from surplus areas to others within the province along the newly developed rail net work : 230 ; see also Kessinger, 85.

[10] *Census Punjab 1921*, pt II, 2.

[11] *Census Punjab 1911*, pt II, 243-88.

[12] Mitra, Vol II, 793.

[13] The percentage of decrease was 13.98 in Amritsar, 14.42 in Jalandhar, 11.01 in Gurdaspur, and 6.60 in Sialkot: *Census Punjab 1911*, pt II, 2.

[14] *Census Punjab 1921*, pt I, 15; pt II, 2.

annual rate of increase of 1.4 per cent or 14.16 per cent for the decade. The artisan castes, however, registered an increase of .36 per cent per annum and 3.61 per cent during the decade and the total figure reached to 18.4 lacs.[15]

The comparison between the total population figures and those for the artisan castes indicates two different tendencies. The artisans broadly conformed to the general population trends during 1881-1911, though they increased or decreased at rates higher than those for the former. The number of the artisans increased at much lower rate during 1911-1931. The higher rate of increase among them in the previous period, that is during 1881-1901, may be attributed to the generally high fertility rate among the people with smaller income.[16]

The higher rate of decline in the population of the artisan castes during 1901-1911 can perhaps be explained in terms of the exceptionally high rate of mortality caused by natural calamities, combined with the prevailing socio-economic conditions in villages and towns. The artisans were generally the first among the villagers who were affected by any scarcity created by famines, floods, droughts or by the outbreak of epidemics. At such times, the land-owners did not have enough for their own use what to talk of paying to the *kamins* their usual share of the produce. Since the artisans were generally living from hand to mouth and were entirely dependent on cultivators for their sustenance, they were unable to tide over such exceptional situations. Nor could they migrate to urban areas in large numbers as there were not many opportunities for them yet. Hence, the higher rate of mortality among them.[17]

In urban areas the artisans tenaciously clung to their callings but here too there was a noticeable decline in their per capita income. Their already meagre income did not increase despite the rise in prices during the period.[18] The insanitary

[15] *Census Punjab 1931,* pt I, 18; pt II, 2, 285-301.

[16] Sidhu, 57-63, 64 and Heer, 52-53, 62-63.

[17] *Famine Commission Report 1878-79*, Vol VI, 10-19.

[18] The rise in prices between 1890 and 1910 also was over 35 per cent; but the wages of the artisans did not increase at all: Wilson, 14; Sharma

living conditions would also account for higher death rate among the urban artisans.[19]

With regard to the lower rate of growth among the artisans during 1911-31, it may be pointed out that within the lower income group the rate of both fertility and mortality has generally been higher. The higher mortality has been due to their low level of nutrition and unhygienic conditions of living.[20] In addition, the number of dependents per working artisan also increased during 1901-21, which further affected their living conditions. The number of actual workers among the potters, for instance, declined by 1.76 per cent from 1901 to 1921, but the number of dependents among them increased by 11 per cent. Similarly, the shoe-makers increased by 81 per cent and their dependents by 87 per cent during the same period. Among the weavers the number of actual workers declined by 15.52 per cent during 1911-21, whereas that of their dependents decreased by 10.60 per cent only. The tanners too fared similarly. Comparison between the data for

TABLE I

		Census Year		*Per cent increase or decrease*
	1901	*1911*	*1921*	
Potters				
Actual Workers	40,504	40,956	39,790	−1.76
Dependents	81,164	83,139	90,246	+11.18
Shoe makers				
Actual Workers	59,678	75,678	1,08,185	+81.28
Dependents	1,14,819	1,36,273	2,14,806	+87.28
Weavers				
Actual Workers	—	1,96,782	1,66,223	−15.52
Dependents	—	2,75,741	2,59,492	−10.60
Tanners				
Actual Workers	41,631	18,043	10,578	−74.59
Dependents	60.699	35,860	22,994	−62.20

(1983), 509-10.

[19] See *Census Punjab 1891*, pt I, 72.

[20] See Sidhu, 35; Heer, 62-63.

actual workers and their dependents in the table I brings out the point more sharply.[21]

Thus, the increase in the number of dependents on almost stagnant wages contributed towards the decline in per capita income and further towards malnutrition, inability to resist diseases, and to a larger number of deaths than the surviving births.

It is not surprising, therefore, that the proportion of the artisans to the total population also continued to decline from 1911 onwards. In 1911, the percentage of the artisan castes in total population was 17.41 which declined to 16.54 in 1921 and 14.88 in 1931.[22] This was despite increase in their absolute numbers, from 17.5 lacs in 1911 to 18.4 lacs in 1931. But as already mentioned, the rate of increase was far below the general rate of increase. Whereas the increase in the total population during 1911-31 was 23.58 per cent, the population of artisan castes increased by only 5.61 per cent.[23]

III

There was less discrepency between the district wise population figures and the distribution of artisans in different districts from 1881 to 1931. The most populous districts throughout the period of colonial rule were Hoshiarpur, Jalandhar, Ferozepur, Lahore, Amritsar, Gurdaspur and Sialkot

[21] Data adapted from: *Census Punjab 1901*, pt II, 304-08; *Census Punjab 1911*, pt II, 291-311; *Census Punjab 1921*, pt II, 156.

[22] Proportion of artisan castes to the total population was 17.50 in 1881, 17.83 in 1891 and 17.91 in 1901: *Census Punjab 1881*, pt II, Table VIII-A; *Census Punjab 1911*, pt II, 243-88; *Census Punjab 1921*, pt II, 207-52; *Census Punjab 1931*, pt II, 285-301.

[23] Percentage increase and decrease of the population of artisan castes between 1881 and 1931:

Period	Change
1881 - 1891	+14.40
1891 - 1901	+10.22
1901 - 1911	−6.78
1911 - 1921	+1.93
1921 - 1931	+3.61

Based on the sources mentioned in n.22 above

with a percentage of the total population varying between 9 and 11. This percentage ranged between 5 and 8 in the districts of Ludhiana, Gujranwala and Gujrat.[24] The district of Lyallpur, however, deserves reference. In the areas covered by this district the population was even less than 5 per cent of the total in 1881, yet it rose to 5 per cent of the total in 1891 and to over 9 per cent of the total in 1931. This exceptional increase was due to the establishment of canal colonies, because a large number of people migrated from other areas of the Punjab to settle in this district. The table II adds further.

Turning to the figures for the artisan castes in 1881, they formed around 20 per cent of the population in the districts of Hoshiarpur, Jalandhar, Ludhiana and Gujranwala, and between 15 and 18 per cent in the districts of Lahore, Amritsar, Gurdaspur, Sialkot, Gujrat and Jhang. As evident from the figures in table III there was not an exact correspondence between the most populous districts and those with the maximum concentration of the artisan castes. This could be explained with reference primarily to two factors : one the concentration of large number of towns, including the cities of Amritsar and Lahore, in the upper Bari, upper Rachna and the Chaj Doabs. Secondly the two cities accounted for a much larger population of the districts, while the artisans were scattered mostly in the countryside. The higher urban concentration generally went with the lesser percentage of artisans.[25] The decline in their percentage in the populous districts of central Punjab was due partly also to their migration to the canal colonies to support the agricultural operations there.[26]

[24] For instance, the percentage of the total population in Lahore was 9 in 1881 and 11 in 1931. In Amritsar it was more than 10 in 1881 which decreased to just about 9 in 1931. Similarly in Sialkot the percentage was more than 11 in 1881 and decreased to just above 8 in 1931: *Census Punjab 1881*, pt II, Table VIII-A; *Census Punjab 1931*, pt II, 259.

[25] For a discussion of urbanization in the region see Reeta Grewal (1984).

[26] From 1921 to 1931 about 17,000 persons belonging to Chamar, Julaha and Kumhar castes migrated to the Chenab Colony from the districts

The district-wise variations in the proportions of the numerically and otherwise important artisan castes, that is, the Chamar, Mochi, Julaha, Kumhar, Lohar, Tarkhan and the Sunar, also corresponded to the trends evident among the artisans in general. The population of the Julahas, the most numerous among the artisan castes, as the table IV shows, was maximum in the districts of Amritsar, Gurdaspur, Lahore, Sialkot and Gujranwala during the period from 1881 to 1931. In 1881, about 67 per cent of the total Julahas were concentrated in these districts and in 1891, their percentage was over 60. Although the proportion of the Julahas continued to be the largest in these districts, yet it showed slight decrease over the rest of the period; it was 64 per cent in 1901, 65 per cent in 1911, 64 per cent in 1921 and 59 per cent in 1931. The other districts with considerable percentage of the Julahas were Hoshiarpur, Ferozepur and Jhang.

The Kumhars in 1881 were concentrated mainly in the districts of Lahore, Amritsar, Sialkot and Gujranwala with 55 per cent of their total population. In 1901 and 1911, this percentage rose to over 61, but came down to 56 in 1921 and 53 in 1931. The rest of the population as the table V shows was spread more or less evenly in the remaining districts.

The Lohars too tended to concentrate in a few districts, with their largest proportion in Amritsar, Gurdaspur and Sialkot. But their percentage in these districts declined steadily from over 38 in 1881 to 36 in 1891, 35 in 1901 and 31 in 1931. The other districts with substantial number of Lohars, as elaborated in table VI, were Hoshiarpur, Jalandhar, Gujranwala and Gujrat.

The population of the Tarkhans, as the table VII shows, was relatively dense in Amritsar, Gurdaspur Lahore and Sialkot districts. Their percentage in these districts, however, showed some decline from over 47 in 1881 to 35 in 1931. The other districts with sizeable proportion of the Tarkhans were Hoshiarpur, Jalandhar, Ferozepur and Gujranwala.

---

of Hoshiarpur, Jalandhar, Sialkot and Gujranwala: *Census Punjab 1931*, pt II, Table VI-A.

The population of the Sunars, as stated in table VIII was concentrated more in Amritsar, Lahore, and Sialkot districts with around 40 per cent of the total living in these areas in 1881. Their population did increase in terms of absolute figures from 1881 to 1931, but their percentage in these districts declined from 45 in 1891 to 43 in 1901 and 37 in 1921.

Among the leather-workers, the Mochis with more than 50 per cent of their total population were concentrated in the districts of Amritsar, Lahore, Ferozepur, Gujranwala, and Gujrat in 1881. Their percentage in these districts increased to 66 in 1891, but decreased to 58 in 1911 and to 50 in 1931. The table IX gives the details.

The Chamars or the non-Muslim leather-workers had their largest concentration, with more than 82 per cent of their population living in the districts of Hoshiarpur, Jalandhar and Ludhiana in 1881. This percentage was over 81 per cent in 1891 and around 75 in 1931. The table X explains further. It must be noted that more than 62 per cent of the Chamars were concentrated in two districts of Hoshiarpur and Jalandhar. This percentage rose slightly to over 63 in 1891, but fluctuated to 58 in 1901, 54 in 1911 and 50 in 1921, and 60 in 1931. The concentration of the Chamars in Hoshiarpur and Jalandhar districts was said to be due to the conducive conditions for the profession of tanning. The *kikar* tree was found in abundance in this region and its bark was very useful for tanning. There was a large number of cattle in this region and water containing useful ingredients for tanning was easily available. Hides were sent to Jalandhar for tanning from neighbouring areas also.[27]

As already pointed out, it may be difficult to establish an exact correspondence between the artisans belonging to particular castes and the figures for the corresponding occupations. It may, nevertheless, be relevant to point out that among those actually engaged in the artisanal occupations, as the table XI shows, the number of weavers, with 1,95,156

[27] Anand, 21.

TABLE II: DISTRICT-WISE VARIATION OF POPULATION (1881–1931)

District	*1881*	*1891*	*1901*	*1911*	*1921*	*1931*	*Per cent increase/ decrease*
Hoshiarpur	9,01,044	10,11,455	9,89,738	9,18,569	9,27,419	10,32,187	+14.55
Jalandhar	7,89,555	9,07,533	9,17,587	8,01,920	8,22,544	9,43,721	+19.52
Ludhiana	6,18,835	6,48,722	6,73,097	5,17,192	5,67,622	6,72,494	+8.67
Ferozepur	7,47,370	8,85,536	9,57,178	9,59,657	10,98,248	11,56,732	+54.77
Lahore	7,68,873	9,00,012	10,05,205	10,00,855	11,31,336	13,78,570	+79.29
Amritsar	8,93,380	9,92,350	10,23,985	8,83,796	9,29,374	11,17,120	+25.04
Gurdaspur	8,23,695	9,43,922	9,40,334	8,36,771	8,52,192	9,70,898	+17.87
Sialkot	9,40,832	10,27,275	9,96,940	9,31,181	9,37,823	9,79,617	+ 4.12
Gujranwala	5,79,258	6,61,232	7,39,546	6,05,582	6,23,581	7,36,138	+27.08
Sheikhupura	2,88,043	3,34,311	4,28,864	4,36,463	5,23,135	6,96,732	+141.88
Gujrat	7,27,044	8,06,382	7,92,159	7,87,999	8,24,046	9,22,427	+26.87
Lyallpur	40,579	30,136	5,89,009	8,47,862	9,79,463	11,51,351	+185.20
Jhang	3,90,630	4,02,341	4,26,225	5,24,803	5,70,559	6,64,833	+70.19

Data adapted from: *Census Punjab 1881*, pt II, Table II; *Census Punjab 1891*, pt II, 16; *Census Punjab 1901*, pt II, Table I; *Census Punjab 1911*, pt II, Table I; *Census Punjab 1921*, pt II, Table I; *Census Punjab 1931*, pt II, 1.

TABLE III: VARIATION IN THE PERCENTAGES OF ARTISANS CASTES (1881–1931)

District	*1881*	*1891*	*1901*	*1911*	*1921*	*1931*
Hoshiarpur	21.95	22.92	23.42	23.52	20.24	20.51
Jalandhar	21.64	23.17	22.23	21.87	18.76	18.10
Ludhiana	20.04	20.19	20.07	20.04	19.05	15.95
Ferozepur	13.49	16.95	16.92	16.94	16.64	14.68
Lahore	18.68	18.08	17.94	14.56	13.74	12.34
Amritsar	17.74	18.17	18.21	17.27	15.84	14.30
Gurdaspur	17.65	17.93	16.58	17.83	16.79	12.89
Sialkot	15.86	16.04	16.04	15.58	13.95	13.57
Gujranwala	20.88	19.97	20.11	27.67	18.55	17.03
Gujrat	15.59	14.90	14.97	14.94	15.18	14.60
Lyallpur	–	–	–	12.10	14.95	11.57
Jhang	17.08	20.72	17.56	15.90	18.69	17.41

Percentages calculated on the basis of: *Census Punjab 1881* pt II, Table VIII–A; *Census Punjab 1891*, pt II, 630–697; *Census Punjab 1901*, pt II, Table XIII; *Census Punjab 1911*, pt II, Table XIII; *Census Punjab 1921*, pt II, Table XIII; *Census Punjab 1931*, pt II, 285–301.

TABLE IV: DISTRICT-WISE VARIATION OF POPULATION OF JULAHAS (1881–1931)

District	*1881*	*1891*	*1901*	*1911*	*1921*	*1931*	*Per cent increase/ decrease 1881–1931*
Hoshiarpur	20,841	20,412	23,605	21,422	21,669	22,382	+7.35
Jalandhar	15.790	15,964	16,465	13,208	13,690	13,036	–17.44
Ludhiana	14,728	16,537	16,736	11,066	12,198	13,315	–9.59
Ferozepur	20,434	24,394	23,450	22,390	24,480	24,843	+21.57
Lahore	35,742	39,113	44,092	36,427	38,132	41,496	+16.09
Amritsar	41,598	45,864	46,324	36,474	38,182	42,684	+ 2.61
Gurdaspur	40,456	47,955	47,274	40,786	40,746	44,441	+9.85
Sialkot	27,140	29,117	27,694	25,319	23,142	22,608	–16.69
Gujranwala	26,230	27,679	31,070	34,323	21,150	24,375	– 7.07
Sheikhupura	–	–	–	–	16,160	18,553	+14.85
Gujarat	23,870	24,821	22,514	22,331	23,049	24,688	+ 3.42
Lyallpur	–	–	19,932	18,462	23,803	27,628	+ 38.61
Jhang	24,176	28,156	23,736	31,832	34,690	36,102	+49.32

Data adapted from: *Census Punjab 1881*, pt II, Table VIII–A; *Census Punjab 1891*, pt II, 316–318, *Census Punjab 1901*, pt II, Table XIII; *Census Punjab 1911*, pt II, 258; *Census Punjab 1921*, pt II, 222; *Census Punjab 1931*, pt II, 291.

TABLE V: DISTRICT-WISE VARIATION OF POPULATION OF KUMHARS

District	*1881*	*1891*	*1901*	*1911*	*1921*	*1931*	*Per cent increase/ decrease*
Hoshiarpur	10,661	12,213	11,278	9,690	6,435	10,268	−3.69
Jalandhar	12,904	14,475	14,685	12,852	13,370	14,400	+11.59
Ludhiana	8,226	9,544	9,674	7,232	8,397	8,991	+9.30
Ferozepur	15,254	28,105	34,564	37,355	41,473	40,772	+171.33
Lahore	31,524	36,416	40,252	32,156	35,231	37,305	−18.34
Amritsar	29,175	32,639	35,389	31,344	33,437	37,265	+27.73
Gurdaspur	17,029	20,299	21,515	19,263	19,569	21,505	+26.28
Sialkot	29,713	32,028	31,930	30,045	27,897	27,191	−8.49
Gujranwala	26,931	29,231	32,646	38,393	28,734	31,464	+16.83
Sheikhupura	–	–	–	–	19,077	21,817	–
Gujrat	16,401	17,846	17,593	17,638	19,323	21,682	+32.20
Lyallpur	–	–	18,982	16,911	17,678	20,522	+ 8.11
Jhang	15,381	19,459	17,330	22,392	24,685	30,009	+95.69

Data adapted from: *Census Punjab 1881*, Vol II, VIII–A, *Census Punjab, 1891*, pt II, 328–31; *Census Punjab 1901*, pt II, XIII–XVII; *Census Punjab 1911*, pt II, 266–67; *Census Punjab 1921*, pt II, 230; *Census Punjab 1931*, pt II, 293.

TABLE VI: DISTRICT-WISE VARIATION OF POPULATION OF LOHARS

District	*1881*	*1891*	*1901*	*1911*	*1921*	*1931*	*Per cent increase/ decrease*
Hoshiarpur	15,033	16,552	15,906	13,685	9,319	9,618	−36.02
Jalandhar	13,396	15,548	15,477	13,524	8,174	7,454	− 44.36
Ludhiana	8,520	8,517	8,727	6,108	5,330	5,148	−39.15
Ferozepur	7,097	16,471	9,839	9,082	10,794	10,784	+51.95
Lahore	37,767	16,238	16,548	14,550	15,414	16,820	+22.18
Amritsar	18,778	21,758	22,130	18,917	18,384	19,523	+3.97
Gurdaspur	16,601	17,038	16,750	14,242	12,637	11,657	− 29.78
Sialkot	18,584	20,762	21,266	18,002	17,214	17,162	−7.65
Gujranwala	12,364	13,664	15,838	15,708	12,394	13,828	+11.84
Sheikhupura	–	–	–	–	6,245	8,257	–
Gujrat	12,934	–	13,582	13,421	13,851	14,542	+12.43
Lyallpur	–	–	8,406	9,391	11,388	11,434	+ 36.02
Jhang	3,062	4,144	3,535	4,717	5,086	5,520	+ 80.27

Data adapted from: *Census Punjab 1881*, pt II, VIII–A; *Census Punjab 1891*, pt II, 674–727; *Census Punjab 1901*, pt II, XIII; *Census Punjab 1911*, pt II, 268–69; *Census Punjab 1921*, pt II, 232; *Census Punjab 1931*, pt II, 293.

TABLE VII: DISTRICT-WISE VARIATION OF POPULATION OF TARKHANS

District	*1881*	*1891*	*1901*	*1911*	*1921*	*1931*	*Per cent increase/ decrease*
Hoshiarpur	28,033	30,342	33,811	32,395	19,433	39,535	+41.03
Jalandhar	26,232	39,622	32,160	29,267	14,531	19,463	−25.80
Ludhiana	18,809	19,182	20,994	17,258	16,300	18,788	+0.36
Ferozepur	21,424	28,380	31,114	31,670	34,575	29,493	+37.66
Lahore	31,009	36,741	40,220	34,287	34,674	42,288	+36.37
Amritsar	34,944	38,731	41,025	33,494	26,753	25,099	+28.17
Gurdaspur	29,621	35,142	35,276	30,226	25,472	21,374	− 27.84
Sialkot	41,781	44,387	43,967	40,359	36,222	39,931	−4.42
Gujranwala	26,872	29,236	32,693	35,166	27,033	26,207	−2.47
Sheikhupura	–	–	–	–	14,475	14,563	–
Gujrat	21,828	23,155	24,155	23,600	25,544	28,659	+31.29
Lyallpur	–	–	16,664	16,706	18,455	19,697	+18.09
Jhang	8,418	11,058	10,445	13,224	14,463	15,368	+ 82.56

Data adapted from: *Census Punjab 1881*, pt II, VIII A; *Census Punjab 1891*, pt II, 784–97; *Census Punjab 1901*, pt II, XIII; *Census Punjab 1911*, pt II, 287; *Census Punjab 1921*, pt II, 251–52; *Census Punjab 1931*, pt II, 301.

TABLE VIII: DISTRICT–WISE VARIATION OF POPULATION OF SUNARS

District	*1881*	*1891*	*1901*	*1911*	*1921*	*1931*	*Per cent increase/ decrease*
Hoshiarpur	6,689	7,342	7,494	6,139	1,885	5,528	−17.35
Jalandhar	6,900	8,922	9,343	7,582	2,437	7,633	+10.62
Ludhiana	5,962	6,178	6,888	4,872	4,269	5,071	−14.96
Ferozepur	4,812	7,264	7,962	7,124	7,687	8,097	+68.26
Lahore	8,317	9,065	8,978	6,196	6,304	6,330	−23.89
Amritsar	8,605	9,464	10,952	6,949	4,352	7,160	−16.79
Gurdaspur	6,008	7,172	7,292	6,196	4,764	6,147	+2.31
Sialkot	8,947	9,815	10,065	8,601	4,184	6,383	−28.65
Gujranwala	6,141	7,129	8,069	7,080	4,841	4,669	−23.97
Sheikhupura	–	–	–	–	3,136	3,241	–
Gujrat	5,446	5,862	6,041	5,757	5,162	5,348	−1.79
Lyallpur	–	–	3,384	4,904	4,942	5,014	+48.16
Jhang	1,697	2,996	3,492	3,599	3,685	2,700	+59.10

Data adapted from: *Census Punjab 1881*, pt II, VIII–A; *Census Punjab 1891*, pt II, 714–27; *Census Punjab* , pt II, XIII; *Census Punjab 1911*, pt II, 274; *Census Punjab 1921*. pt II, 237; *Census Punjab 1931*, pt II, 295.

TABLE IX: DISTRICT-WISE VARIATION OF POPULATION OF MOCHIS

District	*1881*	*1891*	*1901*	*1911*	*1921*	*1931*	*Per cent increase/ decrease*
Hoshiarpur	14,726	18,778	17,296	14,903	14,993	16,055	+9.02
Jalandhar	16,517	19,968	19,745	17,703	18,328	17,233	+4.33
Ludhiana	8,171	9,271	9,233	6,409	6,349	6,648	–18.63
Ferozepur	18,386	22,097	22,905	22,884	24,384	24,612	+33.86
Lahore	18,527	22,195	23,892	18,092	20,032	22,227	+19.97
Amritsar	24,311	30,600	28,919	23,379	23,882	26,400	+8.59
Gurdaspur	14,716	17,466	15,347	14,416	14,702	16,159	+9.80
Sialkot	15,003	15,916	16,844	14,798	13,574	13,124	–12.55
Gujranwala	22,260	24,921	28,017	30,350	20,938	24,454	+9.85
Sheikhupura	–	–	–	–	13,525	16,640	–
Gujrat	32,461	34,910	34,078	34,229	36,458	38,459	+18.47
Lyallpur	–	–	16,129	17,109	19,240	21,649	+34.22
Jhang	14,132	17,555	16,323	20,737	23,945	25,426	+79.91

Data adapted from: *Census Punjab 1881*, pt II, VIII–A; *Census Punjab 1891*, pt II, 714–27; *Census Punjab 1901*, pt II, xiii-xxi; *Census Punjab 1911*, pt II, 274; *Census Punjab 1921*, pt II, 237; *Census Punjab 1931*, pt II, 295.

TABLE X: DISTRICT-WISE VARIATION OF POPULATION OF CHAMARS

District	*1881*	*1891*	*1901*	*1911*	*1921*	*1931*	*Per cent increase/ decrease*
Hoshiarpur	1,00,207	1,24,578	1,21,003	1,17,844	1,14,034	1,08,380	+8.15
Jalandhar	79,155	95,874	96,191	81,256	83,803	91,643	+15.77
Ludhiana	59,655	61,817	62,875	50,720	55,312	49,315	−17.33
Ferozepur	13,501	22,935	32,182	32,134	39,447	31,293	+131.78
Lahore	4,775	3,024	1,923	4,071	5,673	3,729	−21.90
Amritsar	1,049	1,348	1,784	2,094	2,319	1,967	+29.52
Gurdaspur	20,972	24,230	27,561	24,099	25,248	3,931	—
Sialkot	8,076	12,791	8,157	8,045	8,639	6,594	−18.35
Gujranwala	183	831	405	6,579	630	404	+120.76
Sheikhupura	–	–	–	–	8,396	6,748	—
Gujrat	440	614	632	787	1,164	1,380	+213.63
Lyallpur	–	–	27,220	34,335	50,948	27,330	+.42
Jhang	34	47	—	181	100	571	–

Data compiled on the basis of: *Census Punjab 1881*, pt II, Table VIII–A; *Census Punjab 1891*, pt II, 273–74; *Census Punjab 1901*, pt II, XIII; *Census Punjab 1911*, pt II, 243; *Census Punjab 1921*, pt II, 207; *Census Punjab 1931*, pt II, 285.

TABLE XI: NUMBER OF WORKERS IN DIFFERENT OCCUPATIONS

Occupation	*1881*	*1891*	*1901*	*1911*	*1921*	*1931*
Weavers	2,00,655	4,91,872	1,95,156	2,38,907	1,66,223	1,62,622
Carpenters	53,590	1,23,285	42,478	70,995	74,139	87,628
Tanners	7,530	11,610	41,631	18,043	10,578	6,500
Ironsmiths	28,916	69,920	26,504	31,836	31,823	41,101
Potters	40,523	99,229	40,504	40,956	39,790	48,093
Shoemakers	71,618	2,29,986	59,678	75,676	1,08,185	92,858
Goldsmiths	22,527	78,604	26,240	29,526	26,330	26,063

There is little correspondence between the figures for 1881 and 1891

Data adapted from: *Census Punjab 1881*, pt II,Table XII A–B; *Census Punjab 1891*, pt II, 416; *Census Punjab 1901*, pt II, Table XV; *Census Punjab 1911*, pt II, 304–8; *Census Punjab 1921*, pt II, 291–311; *Census Punjab 1931*, pt II, 156–84.

persons was the largest in 1901. In 1911, their number rose to 2,38,907 but came down to 1,62,622 in 1931. The leather-workers were next to the weavers in number. In 1901, their number was more than 59,000 and was around 92,000 in 1931. In 1911, the carpenters numbered nearly 71,000 and rose to over 74,000 in 1921 and over 87,000 in 1931. The number of potters was over 40,000 in 1901 and around 48,000 in 1931. The blacksmiths were another major occupational group with their number around 26,000 in 1901 and 41,000 in 1931. The number of the goldsmiths was around 26,000 in the Punjab in 1901 which rose to 29,000 in 1911 and again came down to around 26,000 in 1931. In 1901, among the 'actual workers' enumerated as the 'servants' of the village societies, were over 34,000 tanners, 24,000 carpenters, 18,000 potters, 16,000 blacksmiths and 12,000 shoe-makers. They formed nearly 48 per cent of the total of 'actual workers' engaged in different artisanal occupations.[28]

IV

Religion-wise composition of artisan castes may also be of some interest. In 1881, the Muslims constituted about 55 per cent and in 1931, 56 per cent of the total population of the Punjab.[29] Among the artisans too, they constituted the dominant section with 57 per cent of the total; their population increased from 8.49 lacs in 1881 to 14.11 lacs in 1931.[30] Increase in the number of Muslims seems to be due

[28] *Census Punjab 1901,* pt II, Table XV.

[29] *Census Punjab 1881*, pt II, 1-2; *Census Punjab 1931*, pt II, Table II.

[30] The number of Muslims among the artisan castes:

Year	*Total Number*	*Percentage*
1881	8,49,636	57.05
1891	9,91,016	58.16
1901	10,93,409	58.22
1911	10,14,814	57.97
1921	10,78,412	60.43
1931	14,11,707	76.36

Source: *Census Punjab 1881*, pt II, Table VIII; *Census Punjab 1891*, pt II,

largely to natural increase rather than proselytization.[31] The Julaha, Kumhar, Lohar and the Mochi castes were predominantly Muslim. More than 98 per cent of the Mochis, 95 per cent Julahas, 70 per cent Kumhars and 60 to 80 per cent of the Lohars were Muslims. This percentage was rather small in case of the Sunars and the Tarkhans. In 1881, the percentage of Hindus in the total population was 37 and among the artisans, it was 32. The number of Hindus among the artisan castes declined from 4.79 lacs in 1881 to 2.26 lacs in 1931.[32] This steep fall was caused mainly in 1931 when more than 2.14 lacs of Chamars were enumerated as the Ad-Dharmis.[33] Earlier the percentage of Hindus among the Chamars was 90 in 1881 and 83 in 1921. Among the Sunars also the percentage of Hindus declined from 66 in 1881 to 54 in 1931. Increase in the number of the Sikhs among the artisans was yet another reason for the decline in their numbers among Hindus.

Sikhs constituted 6 per cent of the total population and the artisan castes among them constituted 11 per cent in 1881.

639-97; *Census Punjab 1901*, pt II, Table XIII; *Census Punjab 1911*, pt II, 243-48; *Census Punjab 1921*, pt II, 207-52; *Census Punjab 1931*, pt II, 285-301.

[31] See Lavan, 10.

Incidentally, the higher proportion of the artisans among the Punjabi Muslims also points to the general backwardness of the community in the province.

[32] The number of Hindus among the artisan castes:

Year	*Total*	*Percentage*
1881	4,79,127	32.17
1891	5,23,614	30.73
1901	5,67,765	30.23
1911	4,69,438	26.81
1921	4,89,460	27.43
1931	2,26,400	12.24

Source: *Census Punjab 1881*, pt II, Table VIII-A; *Census Punjab 1891*, pt II, 630-97; *Census Punjab 1901*, pt II, Table XIII; *Census Punjab 1911*, pt II, 243-48; *Census Punjab 1921*, pt II, 209-52; *Census Punjab 1931*, pt II, 285-301.

[33] See Juergensmeyer, 45-46; also Sharma (1983), 136, and chapter seven below.

TABLE XII: RELIGION–WISE COMPOSITION OF ARTISAN CASTES (PERCENTAGES ONLY)

Caste/Religion	*1881*	*1891*	*1901*	*1911*	*1921*	*1931*
Chamar						
Hindu	90.98	85.90	83.52	82.44	83.44	21.79
Sikh	8.59	11.81	7.15	17.53	16.16	13.06
Muslim	.42	2.59	9.32	–	.39	(64.56 Ad–Dharmi)
Julaha						
Hindu	1.89	2.08	2.23	3.26	2.79	6.12
Sikh	.73	.58	1.16	1.22	1.10	.93
Muslim	97.37	97.33	96.60	95.51	95.10	92.94
Kumhar						
Hindu	20.75	12.97	21.79	19.41	18.62	15.84
Sikh	3.03	3.84	6.49	6.31	7.87	7.67
Muslim	76.71	83.19	71.71	74.27	73.50	76.48
Lohar						
Hindu	25.45	19.71	19.24	11.64	16.96	7.67
Sikh	11.88	12.40	17.05	18.06	9.99	7.89
Muslim	62.66	67.88	63.71	70.29	73.04	85.43

contd. . . .

1	*2*	*3*	*4*	*5*	*6*	*7*
Mochi						
Muslim	99.95	99.15	99.22	98.82	98.78	98.51
Sunar						
Hindu	66.85	66.11	66.85	56.90	54.49	53.70
Sikh	14.70	12.84	16.64	29.52	21.58	24.71
Muslim	18.44	21.04	16.50	13.57	23.92	21.58
Tarkhan						
Hindu	29.27	21.90	24.17	13.81	12.45	8.73
Sikh	26.69	31.44	28.92	39.11	32.00	31.80
Muslim	44.03	46.65	46.90	47.07	55.54	59.46

Percentages calculated on the basis of: *Census Punjab 1881*,pt. II, Table VIII–A; *Census Punjab 1891,* pt II, 630–797; *Census Punjab 1901*, pt II, Table XIII; *Census Punjab 1911*, pt II, 243–88; *Census Punjab 1921*, pt II, Table V; *Census Punjab 1931*, pt II, 285– 301.

The number of Sikhs among the artisans rose from 1.60 lacs in 1881 to 2.10 lacs in 1931.[34] This increase though significant in terms of absolute numbers, was not very substantial in terms of percentages. Sikhs had their significant percentage among the Tarkhans and the Sunars; it was 26 in 1881 and nearly 32 in 1931 among the Tarkhans, and nearly 15 in 1881 and 24 in 1931 among the Sunars. Their percentage among the Chamars was 8 in 1881 and 12 in 1931. The table XII elaborates further. In addition to the natural increase, it could perhaps be attributed partly to the socio-religious reform movemen ts among the Sikhs, like the Nirankari, the Namdhari and the Singh Sabha which brought about a qualitative change in the social and economic position of the artisan castes.

[34] The number of Sikhs among the artisan castes:

Year	*Total Number*	*Percentage*
1881	1,60,424	10.77
1891	1,89,050	11.09
1901	2,16,697	11.54
1911	2,66,211	15.20
1921	2,16,416	12.12
1931	2,10.595	11.39

Source: *Census Punjab 1881*, pt II, Table VIII; *Census Punjab 1891*, pt II, 639- 97; *Census Punjab 1901*, pt II, Table XIII; *Census Punjab 1911*, pt II, 243-48; *Census Punjab 1921*, pt II, 207-52; *Census Punjab 1931*, pt II, 285-301.

CHAPTER FOUR

Sources and Mechanics of Change

The Punjab had been experiencing social mobility in the wake of the Sikh movement and the decline of the Mughal empire.[1] With its annexation to the British empire in 1849 it came to witness those innovations in the political, administrative, economic and social spheres which had already swept the rest of the country.[2] The new influences gradually undermined the traditional institutions and customary obligations and it became possible for individuals and groups to change their hereditary occupations and consequently their social standing. Sources and mechanics of change in the Punjab, having a bearing on the position of artisans can be studied with reference to the processes in the spheres of agrarian and urban economy, transport and communications, education and socio-religious reform. These changes produced gradual alterations and readjustments over an extended period of time, because the artisans were slow in their response. Most of the changes in social and economic relationships, nevertheless, became evident during the early twentieth century.

I

The agrarian society received the immediate attention of the British administrators who believed that the landholders who dominated the rural society could provide a stable and loyal

[1] Banga (1980), 125-37.

[2] On the developments in political and economic spheres and their implications for different sections of society see Dharma Kumar (1965), Ravinder Kumar (1968).

base in the Punjab.[3] More than 80 per cent of the population of the Punjab was dependent upon agriculture.[4] The province was mainly the land of small cultivators most of whom were the peasant-proprietors who cultivated their own land. For instance, in 1860 in Amritsar, Gurdaspur and Sialkot districts the average holding was 15 acres and the total number of proprietors was 1,94,052 out of whom 1,83,183 or 94.39 per cent were the peasant-proprietors.[5] There were nearly two million peasant-proprietors in the whole of the Punjab in 1872. The number of non-cultivating large landholders in the Punjab unlike some other parts of north India was strikingly small. They numbered 3,661 only.[6] The ground work for the system of land tenures in which the same man was usually the proprietor as well as the cultivator was, in fact, prepared in the Punjab in the period immediately preceding British rule. The rulers in the late eighteenth and early nineteenth century were more favourably inclined towards the actual tillers of the soil, whether self-cultivating proprietors or tenant-cultivators. The agrarian policies of the British government further strengthened the position of the self-cultivating proprietors and vested landed rights in the actual tillers of the soil through various enactments, even the tenants got a legal recognition and a bargaining power that they did not enjoy before.[7] Encouraged by this policy of the state, the traditionally servile sections of the society, like the blacksmiths, carpenters and potters, also began turning to agriculture. For instance, in the three parganas of Amritsar district of the Punjab—Amritsar, Sourian, and Tarn Taran—one-third of the blacksmiths, carpenters, potters and a little more than one-fifth of the shoemakers and weavers were pursuing agriculture as their

[3] Dungen (1972), 299; Imran Ali, 63.

[4] In 1881, 81.75 per cent of those actually engaged in gainful economic activity were agriculturists in one capacity or the other: *Census Punjab 1881*, pt II, Table XII-A.

[5] Cust, Appendices XVI-A and XVIII.

[6] *Punjab Administration Report 1872-73,* 10, 15.

[7] See Banga (1978), 110-11, 168-87; Donin, 31-47, 82-83, Kessinger, 29-31.

occupation during the early nineteenth century.[8]

The British administrators realized the great agricultural potential of the Punjab with its vast uncultivated plains, under-utilized water resources and industrious peasantry. During the period of regency (1845-1849) the early surveyors estimated that 'probably not a fourth of the culturable area was under cultivation' and considerable proportion of the culturable land was lying waste.[9] The new rulers sought to open the province as a market for the produce of British labour and develop it into a major supplier of raw materials and food stuffs to meet the growing requirements of industrial capitalism in Britain.[10] To mobilize the agricultural potentials of the Punjab the British encouraged the cultivators to adopt new varieties of crops and new cropping pattern, besides new implements made of iron and aluminium for the persian wheel, sugar-cane press and the plough.[11] For the preservation and increase in the productive power of the soil the devastating activities of the *chos* or the intermittent hill streams and the resultant water-logging too were checked.[12]

The major contribution to agricultural production, however, was in the sphere of irrigation schemes to utilize the

[8] Radha Sharma, 81-86.

[9] *Foreign/Secret Consultations, April 1848,* No. 60.

The total area of the Punjab in 1855 was 5,22,40,170 acres out of which 1,27,51,161 acres were under cultivation and 54,60,301 acres could be immediately brought under cultivation: *Selections from the Records of the Government of India No. XVIII,* 31.

[10] Domin, 24-25.

[11] These 'judicious measures' were taken to 'increase agricultural produce of the Punjab in quantity and improved in quality to the immediate benefit of the people and for the ultimate advantage of the government': *Progs. Agri-Horticulture Society of the Punjab, August 9,1853.* A similar view was expressed in another communication from the Secretary, Chief Commissioner Punjab on August 19, 1853: *Correspondence on the Improvement of Agriculture in the Punjab by Introduction of European Models, Dated 8 December 1853. F.C. Progs. (Foreign) Govt. of India.* file no.204-206.

[12] The hill torrents from Siwalik range used to cause extensive damage in the districts of Jalandhar, Hoshiarpur and Ambala: *Selections from the Records of the Government of Punjab No. XV,* 2-19.

water resources of the rivers of the Punjab.[13] The Upper Bari Doab Canal, irrigating the districts of Amritsar and Lahore, was the first to be constructed after annexation.[14] The subsequent irrigation projects aimed at colonization of the vast tracts of barren lands were in the Chaj, Rachna, and Bari Doabs—popularly named as Lyallpur, Shahpur, Montgomery, Nili Bar and the Ganji Bar colonies.[15] The canal colonies were the 'most potent of the many benefits that the British believed that their rule had brought to the people of the Punjab'. There were nine canal colonies in all, and they absorbed the available lands of the Bari, Rachna, and the Chaj Doabs. The colonies became 'virtual human laboratory as castes, clans and tribes from different parts of the province converged on the new lands and unhinged the traditional moorings of village society, and freed people for intercourse in the wider world'.[16] It became a major demographic outlet for the people in thickly populated districts of the Punjab who moved out to colonies in the newly irrigated areas. The explicit aims for colonization were relief from population congestion, settlement of the land with the most efficient agriculturists from Amritsar, Jalandhar, Ludhiana and Lahore and improvement in standard of living of rural population.[17]

The colonists were divided into three broad categories—the peasants (*abadkars*), the yeomen farmers (*sufedposh*) and the capitalist (*rais*) landlords. The *abadkars* were given from half a square to two squares; the *sufedposh* from two to five squares and the *rais* were granted from six to twenty squares

[13] Imran Ali, 3.

[14] The work on the Upper Bari Doab Canal was started in 1851 and completed in 1859; it irrigated about 93,000 acres of land in 1860- 61. By 1911-12 the canal irrigated an area of 11,57,000 acres of land in Gurdaspur, Amritsar and Lahore districts: Douie (1916),132-33.

[15] The Lower Chenab Colony or the Lyallpur colony, Lower Jhelum Canal Colony or the Montgomery Colony and Nili Bar Colony in the southern parts of Montgomery and Multan districts were totally colonization works whereas the Sutlej valley project was partly so: Imran Ali, 8-61.

[16] Imran Ali, viii.

[17] Imran Ali, 13; *Census Punjab 1881*, pt II, Table I.

of land.[18] The peasant-proprietors formed the most important category of the colonists. The peasant grantees held about 80 per cent of the area in Lyallpur and 59 per cent in Shahpur colonies.[19] They were mainly from the central districts of Amritsar, Lahore, Gujrat, Sialkot, Gurdaspur, Hoshiarpur, Jalandhar and Ludhiana.[20] A large number of artisans accompanied their patrons and settled down in the newly inhabited colonies. For their maintenance the government granted them separate lands.[21] Within first ten years the Chenab Colony alone had attracted a good number of people from among the artisan castes, particularly the Chamars, Kumhars, and the Tarkhans. By 1904, there were, among others, about 20,000 Julahas, 19,000 Kumhars, 17,000 Tarkhans and over 27,000 Chamars.[22] For the artisans the opening of the canal colonies not only meant the extension of village society in the newly settled areas but also the loosening of traditional ties by the movement of the colonists from their old established villages to the new ones.

Colonization was accompanied by the development of the means of transportation—railways and roads. Works on railways and roads progressed more rapidly in the Punjab than other parts of the empire during the late nineteenth century. The newly annexed province had to be linked up with the ports and other important cities. In 1862, the first railway line was opened in the Punjab between Amritsar and Lahore; it was 37 kilometers long.[23] The length of railways increased to 1,689 kilometers in 1881 and to 4,987 kilometers in 1901.[24] Lahore was connected with Multan in 1865 and Amritsar with Delhi in 1870. By the end of the 1870s Amritsar was linked up with Bombay at a distance of 2,016 kilometers, with

[18] Imran Ali, 18-19. A square was equal to nearly 28 acres.

[19] Darling, 117.

[20] *Census Punjab 1931*, pt I, 15-16.

[21] See *Annual Report of Canal Colonies 1903,* 11; ibid. 1904, 1-2.

[22] *Gazetteer Chenab Colony 1904*, 57-58.

[23] The railway line was opened to public on April 10, 1862. The single fare was 4 annas only: *Punjab Administration Report 1861-62*, 74-75.

[24] *Census Punjab 1901*, pt I, 15-16.

Calcutta at a distance of 1,971 kilometers, and with Karachi at a distance of 1,206 kilometers. By 1880, the railways connected Lahore also with several other towns in the south, west and the north. In 1883, the link between Delhi and Peshawar was completed. The branch lines were gradually developed over the following years.[25] By 1916, the major urban centres and the canal colonies of Lyallpur, Sargodha and Multan were connected by railways. By 1939, the length of the railway track connecting all parts of the province was nearly 10,000 kilometers.[26]

The road communication, though much less extensive than the railways, also contributed towards linking different parts of the region. The first step in this direction was the extension of the Grand Trunk Road between Calcutta and Peshawar which ran more or less parallel to the railways. In 1863-64 it passed through the major urban centres in the province, like Karnal, Ambala, Ludhiana, Jalandhar, Amritsar, Lahore, Gujranwala, Rawalpindi and Jhelum.[27] Several feeder roads branched off from the main highway.[28] By 1939, the length of the metalled roads in the province was over 7,000 kilometers.[29] Wheeled traffic in the form of carts, tongas, bicycles, motor cycles, motor lorries, cars and trucks quickened the pace and movement of traffic.[30]

[25] In 1889 Rajpura was connected with Bhatinda; Sialkot and Jammu were connected in 1890; south Punjab main line was completed in 1897: *Census Punjab 1921*, pt I, 16-17.

[26] All India figure for the railway track in 1946-47 was 65,217 kilometers: *Cambridge Economic History of India,* 739; for Punjab see Khosla (1976).

[27] The Grand Trunk Road was metalled throughout its length and was continuously improved by the construction of bridges over rivers and canals and policed for the safe movement of people and goods: Douie (1916), 123-28.

[28] Important among them were between Ludhiana and Malerkotla; between Ludhiana and Ferozepur; between Jalandhar and Hoshiarpur; between Lahore and Ferozepur; between Gujranwala and Sialkot and between Sialkot and Wazirabad: *Census Punjab 1921*, pt I, 17.

[29] Mathur, 106-11; Saini, 301-11.

[30] The motor vehicles, it seems, had been introduced in the Punjab by the early years of the present century. In 1911 there were 146 motor cycles and

Development of transportation system, particularly the railways, led to commercialization of agriculture. The agriculturists now did not cultivate land for home consumption alone. They grew specialized crops such as wheat, cotton, sugarcane and oilseeds on commercial scale for sale in the market. Commercialization progressed rapidly and cotton and wheat became the major items of export from the Punjab.[31] The railways facilitated the transportation of the cash crops to other parts of India, especially to the ports of Bombay, Karachi, and Calcutta for export. Imported manufactured goods with cotton piece goods as a major item, were brought to the rural areas of the Punjab.[32] The effects of the railways, however, were felt more in towns and villages which were situated along the track or were within the reach of the railway network. At any rate, with the extension of the market economy and the expansion of cash nexus, villages no longer remained the relatively isolated economic units.[33] The inter-communication between villages and urban centres increased with much greater pace than ever before.[34]

In this process, there sprang up a new class of middlemen who started purchasing grain and other products of villages to take to city markets and bring back manufactured goods. These goods replaced the ones manufactured by the village

---

316 lorries which increased to 4,146 motor cycles and nearly 18,000 cars and lorries in 1931. This number was in addition to vehicles maintained by the army and the police: *Census Punjab 1931*, pt I, 50.

[31] The export of wheat was 22.62 lakh maunds in 1884 which increased significantly to over 28.38 lakh quintals in 1904-5: *Progs. Revenue and Agriculture, March 1884,* No. 49-66; Banga (1992), 342. In 1903, for instance, the value of wheat exported from the port of Karachi was 7.5 crores of rupees and that of raw cotton 2.75 crores: Banga (1992), 341.

[32] In 1903-04 the total value of imports through the port of Karachi was 5.9 crores of rupees out of which the value of cotton piece goods was 2 crore rupees: Banga (1992), 341.

[33] Expansion of cash nexus may be guaged from the circulation of currency notes in the Punjab. In 1892 currency notes worth 134 lakhs were in circulation which increased to 263 lakhs in 1903-04: *Imperial Gazetteer 1908,* vol IX, 308.

[34] See for example Eglar, 4; Kessinger, 106.

artisans. The artisans—the potters, carpenters, blacksmiths, leather-workers and the weavers in particular—could not hold out for long against competition with the industrial products thus brought from outside the village.

II

The textile industry which supported the largest number of artisans was perhaps the worst affected of the indigenous manufactures.[35] The inflow of cotton piece goods increased steadily over the years after annexation. By the second decade of colonial rule, the well-to-do agriculturists in villages had begun clothing themselves in English cotton.[36] The administration report of the Punjab for 1861-62 noted that the 'cotton textures of Manchester and other centres of England were fast replacing the native handloom woven clothes'.[37] Till the end of the 1860s the import of cotton cloth in the Punjab was 40,000 maunds a year.[38] By the 1880s, however, this figure increased enormously; the import of cotton cloth between 1881 and 1884 was around 1.1 million maunds valuing over 13 crores of rupees. The value of the imported cotton goods per year was more than the value of the entire output of the indigenous handloom weaving industry of the Punjab.[39] The growing communication network reduced the already limited market for the local weavers. By the beginning of the 1880s the weavers of the Punjab were said to have been 'reduced to poverty in the extreme'.[40] The well-known centres of cotton weaving in the province, in the districts of Gujrat, Ludhiana, Sialkot and Jhang, suffered greatly from

[35] Anstey, 208-09.

[36] *Punjab Administration Report 1861-62,* Appendix IV.

[37] *Punjab Administration Report 1861-62,* xxxvi.

[38] *Punjab Administration Report 1868-69,*113.

[39] The import of cotton cloth in the Punjab in 1881-82 was 3.85 lakh maunds which within the next two years reached to over 4.28 lakh maunds. The total value of these imports in 1884 was 13.63 crore rupees. During these years the value of indigenous production was around worth 10 crore rupees only; *Report on Internal Trade and Manufactures 1883-84,* 3-4.

[40] *Census Punjab 1881*, pt I, 385.

competition with the products injected into its urban and rural markets.[41]

Cotton textile industry did, however, survive but its development was arrested. Only two categories of handloom products could survive: the articles possessing distinctive artistic character and facing no competition, and the coarse cloth in which durability was the primary consideration. The local customs and life styles of rural people also served to sustain the handloom weaving in the Punjab.[42] Cloth was still woven by hand in villages to furnish the local requirements of the poorer sections of the society.[43] At best, the weavers could combine the profession of weaving with agriculture or field labour to make a living. In fact, they were not in a position to compete with machine looms, and to furnish the requirements of wealthier classes according to their new tastes. The setback to hand weaving could not be checked and it was 'hardly possible to do anything to prevent it from declining'.[44]

With the growing interaction between the urban and rural areas the weavers were increasingly becoming dependent on the city market for the sale of their manufactures.[45] By the last quarter of the 19th century, the land-owners had also begun to curtail the remuneration of the weavers. This obliged them to work either independently or for the businessmen in towns and cities who had the greater competence and the means to sell their products.[46] This situation led to the growth of the city based traders as middlemen who purchased all that the

[41] *Report on Internal Trade and Manufactures 1883-84,* 3; *Census Punjab 1901,* pt I, 363.

[42] *D.O. from the Registrar, Home Department, Government of India to the Registrar, Commerce and Industry, Government of India No. 1323, dated 13 September 1905.*

[43] *Census Punjab 1881,* pt I, 358.

[44] Commenting on the condition of the weaving industry, Alfred Chatterton of Madras Weaving School regretted the misery and suffering which 'millions must endure owing to the loss of their livelihood and their utter inability to make up any new occupation': 281.

[45] Trevaskis, 207; Kessinger, 59-60.

[46] Kessinger, 160.

village weavers had to offer for sale in urban markets.[47] The middlemen exploited the dependence of weavers who were already insecure and restless on account of the continuance of the *baqi* arrangements.

The real wages of the weavers were gradually declining even when the prices in general were rising continuously. The average daily wages of the weavers of coarse cloth between 1878 and 1930 virtually did not increase, whereas the prices during the same period increased by about 50 per cent. In 1878 a weaver in Ludhiana earned 2 annas and the average for the central districts of the Punjab was 3 annas a day; in 1929-30 it was 5 to 6 annas a day.[48]

The weavers did not benefit much from the cooperative movement. The number of societies too was very small.[49] These societies about 200 in number, were formed to finance weavers to enable them to purchase raw materials at cheaper rates. But for marketing their manufactures, they had again to depend upon the middlemen. The involvement of the middlemen at the time of purchasing raw-material and competition with machine looms neutralized the advantages of the cooperative movement. The number of those actually engaged in weaving fell significantly between 1881 and 1931; the number of 'actual workers' in weaving in 1930 was 2,43,802 as compared to the figure of 3,87,633 in 1881. In fact, the number of actually operational looms was 1,71,561 which was much less than the number of actual weavers. Nearly 30 per cent of the weavers were working on part time basis by the mid 1930s.[50]

The leather-workers of villages and towns were also experiencing difficulties in the face of the new economic

[47] *Census Punjab 1901*, pt I, 370. See also Badenoch, 5.

[48] The skilled workers, particularly, the silk weavers, however, earned from 10 to 14 annas a day: *Report Banking Enquiry Committee 1929-30*, 291-95; see also *SR Ludhiana 1873-83*, 140; Badenoch, 5.

[49] *Report Banking Enquiry Committee 1929-30*, 78-79; Badenoch, 5.

[50] Out of 2,43,802 weavers 1,86,956 were the whole time weavers and 65,846 were the part timers: *Progs. Department of Industries and Labour (Labour) file no. 354 of 1936*, 4.

conditions. By the 1930s the lorry and the railway had considerably reduced the dependence on horses and horse-driven carts and tongas and hence reduction in the demand for harness and saddlery. The military and police departments also began to curtail their saddlery requirements by adopting mechanical modes of transportation and movement.[51] Furthermore, the demand for European type of footwear was on the increase with which the leather-workers of the Punjab were unable to compete.[52] The factories which earlier used leather beltings replaced those by more durable and cheaper canvass beltings. The increasing demand for leather in the international market added further to the difficulties of the local leather-workers. Almost all the available good quality leather was purchased from the market for export which left the local leather-workers with inferior quality material, rendering them incapable of competing with the market trends.[53] The inadequacy of the financial resources of the Mochis and the Chamars increased their dependence on the middlemen who purchased tanned leather from them at very low rates.[54] They had also to pay commission to the middlemen at the rate of one anna per rupee. Sometimes, the traders in leather sold hides to the leather-worker on the condition that the finished goods would be sold only through them. They also charged one rupee per maund of leather as shop rent.[55]

Gradual increase in the import of dressed leather too affected the tanners adversely. In 1909-10, for instance, about 5,000 maunds of leather was imported into the Punjab which gradually increased to 20,000 maunds by 1936-37. The export of leather from the Punjab correspondingly declined during this period from 26,000 maunds in 1909-10 to 18,000 maunds in 1936-37. In 1928, a village tanning demonstration party was formed to acquaint the tanners with new and

[51] Anand, 19-20.
[52] *Report Banking Enquiry Committee 1929-30*, 305.
[53] Anand, 18-19.
[54] *Report Banking Enquiry Committee 1929-30*, 302, 305-6.
[55] Anand, 34-36.

improved techniques of tanning so as to improve the quality of leather. But practically no step to improve the financial conditions of the workers in leather was taken without which there was little chance of improving the general condition of the Mochis and the Chamars.[56]

III

The complementarity of agriculture and industry in rural areas was disrupted by the new developments, and within half a century of the coming of the British the land-owners began to prefer manufactured goods from the market for cash price. As already noted, at the outset of the colonial rule, the agriculturists were dependent on village artisans for their requirements of the implements of iron and wood, as well as for earthen pots. By the turn of the twentieth century new sugarcane crushing mills, persian wheels, ploughs, fodder-cutters and other implements were available in the market.[57] The new situation resulted in the decline of the regular income of the Tarkhans, Lohars, Kumhars, Mochis and the Chamars. The services of the Tarkhans and Lohars became less remunerative; they were now required for repair work which was paid for in cash or kind at very low rates.[58] The sphere of the Kumhar as a regular *sepidar* was particularly restricted first by the increasing recourse to canal irrigation in those areas where wells were used for irrigation earlier, and secondly by the influx of metal vessels (*tinds*) for the persian wheel and the household utensils replacing earthen wares.[59] At many places, the Chamar's duty as village servant was reduced to

[56] Anand, 18.

[57] In 1930, for instance, the foundries of the town of Batala brought out nearly 19,000 implements of all descriptions and the total number of implements sold in the Punjab was around 30,000: *Census Punjab 1931*, pt I, 35.

[58] Trevaskis, 107.

[59] This was in spite of 117.2 per cent increase in the number of wells for irrigation purposes. The number of wells in the Punjab increased from 1,46,000 to 3,17,000 between 1849 and 1901: Banerjee (1982), 20.

mending old leather articles.[60] By 1890 the Chamars were no longer the regular *sepidars* in the districts of Amritsar, Jalandhar, Gujranwala and Rawalpindi. A large number of them left tanning which was now done by a small number of tanners in urban areas only. The village leather-workers generally made articles from the tanned leather purchased from the market.[61] Also, the *kamins* were no longer allowed to graze their cattle in the village waste. This was noticeable, particularly in Jalandhar and Multan.[62] Such changes were noticed in several other districts of the Punjab.[63]

Wherever the system of *sep* was fully or partly in operation the customary dues in kind were gradually being discarded in favour of cash payments.[64] The village artisans now worked predominantely, though not exclusively, on a cash basis having independent economic relations with the members of the village societies. Cash rates prevailed in at least half of the villages surveyed in the Punjab by the Wages Survey Commision in the beginning of the twentieth century. In one-fourth of the villages partly cash and partly grain rates were prevalent and in only a small proportion of villages the grain rates were continuing.[65] The first regular wages survey of 1912 reported that in 58 per cent villages of the Punjab purely cash rates were in existence. In about 40 per cent of the villages partly cash and partly grain rates and in the remaining 2 per cent villages purely grain rates prevailed.[66] The percentage of villages with cash wages rose further to 61 in

[60] Earlier, the Chamars were entitled to the hides and skins of the dead cattle that belonged to land-owners. The owners were now interested in selling the hides in the market for a cash price: *SR Jalandhar 1880-86*, 87; *SR Sialkot 1895*, 6; *Monograph on Leather Industry*, 4-5; Kessinger, 159.

[61] *Monograph on Leather Industry*, 5.

[62] Banerjee (1977), 304-05.

[63] *Punjab Report in Reply to the Famine Commission 1878-79*, 7, 13; *DG Rawalpindi*, 75; *DG Ludhiana*, 99-100; *DG Jhelum*, 124.

[64] See also Desai, 95.

[65] Wages survey was conducted in 1909 in 4,728 villages of the Punjab: *Report on Moral and Material Progress of the Punjab 1909-11*, 5.

[66] *First Wages Survey 1912, 6.*

1927 and to 67 in 1932. The villages with mixed wages were respectively 38 and 32 per cent and the villages in which wages in kind still prevailed formed just one per cent of the villages surveyed.[67] The only villages which had reported grain wages were in the relatively agriculturally backward, less well connected by the railways and less urbanized districts of Kangra, Gurdaspur, Shahpur, Dera Ghazi Khan and Muzaffarnagar.[68] The breaking up of the traditional relations was, nevertheless, slow. But the artisans had begun to look for other avenues and opportunities provided particularly by factory industry and modern education.

IV

The development of factory industry in the Punjab, on the whole, was characterized by small units with rather limited capital.[69] Cotton weaving was the largest and the most widespread of all manufacturing units in the province. In 1872-73, out of 4,52,286 units, 55.19 per cent were cotton works; 8.13 per cent were wood works and 6.26 per cent were iron works. The number of larger units was 230 with 5,890 operatives employed.[70] However, the large industrial works in the Punjab to justify the label 'factory' during the second half of the 19th century were very few.[71] The definition of a factory according to the Indian Factories Act of 1879 was a place where not less than 100 persons were employed and steam, water or other mechanical power was used. This clause was amended in 1890 as recommended by the Industrial Commission and the term factory for the purposes of

[67] The numbers of villages surveyed was 2,101 and the most common rate of wages was 6 annas as against 8 to 12 annas in 1927: *Fifth Wages Survey 1932*, vi, 4.

[68] *Fifth Wages Survey 1932*, 4.

[69] *Census Punjab 1911*, pt I, 9.

[70] *Punjab Administration Report 1871-72,* Table VI; *Punjab Administration Report*, 1872-73, 92. The number of works enumerated was: cotton, 2,49,618; leather, 42,269; wood, 36,733; and iron, 28,331.

[71] *Punjab Administration Report 1872-73,* 92.

inspection could be applied to a manufacturing unit where fifty or more hands were employed. Later on, the factories employing twenty or more hands were also brought under the purview of the Factories Act.[72] In the Punjab there were only thirty-four factories in 1893 which could be inspected under the Factory Act of 1879, and the number of operatives was 6,324. In 1903 the number of such factories rose to 188 and that of the operatives to 23,128. As the following table indicates the number of 'factories' rose steadily till the outbreak of the World War:[73]

Year	*Factories*	*Operatives*
1903	188	23,128
1904	191	24,593
1905	235	25,775
1907	253	23,286
1908	243	25,600
1909	243	28,679
1914	201	31,243
1915	187	29,720

Majority of the factories processed agricultural or related products including cotton, wheat, rice, tea, leather, wood and silk. For instance, out of 191 factories, under the purview of Indian Factories Act in 1904 the number of cotton ginning mills alone was 114. In 1910, out of 262 factories, 202 were related to the processing of cotton, even as the number of these factories declined in 1915 the number of cotton ginning mills continued to be the largest.[74] There were some

[72] Before the enactment of the Indian Factories Act of 1879, the term factory was used for a place where a certain number of workmen congregated together in the same village or a locality (*mohalla*) and worked together having some system of sharing gross earnings and dividing the labour: *The Imperial Gazetteer XV, 1908*, 246-47.

[73] *Progs. Department of Commerce and Industry (Factories), October 1907,* 3-16; *ibid., December 1908,* 1-18; *ibid. November 1910,* 1-13; *ibid. November 1912,* 1-16; *ibid. May 1917*, 1-19.

[74] The table below substantiates the point further:

government owned and private glass factories, breweries and some iron foundries scattered in different parts of the Punjab.[75] Till the end of World War I, in fact, the government did not take any appreciable step towards the development of modern industry in the province.[76]

During 1921-1931 there was 77.10 per cent increase in the number of industrial units in the province. In 1921 there were 279 factories which increased to 640 in 1930. There were nearly 50,000 operatives in 1930 as against 42,000 in

---

Year	*No. of Factories*	*Number of Factories Processing cotton*
1904	191	114
1907	253	165
1909	245	186
1910	262	202
1912	268	167
1913	224	170
1914	201	149
1915	187	140

Data adapted from: *Progs. Department of Commerce and Industry (Factories), February 1906*, file no. 2 of 1906; *ibid., October 1907,* 3-16; *ibid., December 1908*, 1-18; *ibid., November 1910,* 1-13; *ibid., November 1912,* 1-16; *ibid., May 1917, 1-17.*

[75] In 1915, the number of such factories was 20, out of which 8 were in Lahore, 3 at Amritsar, 4 at Rawalpindi, and one each at Hissar, Karnal and Shimla. These included a railway workshop and an arsenal factory also: *Annual Report on the Working of Indian Factories Act of 1911 in the Punjab for the year 1915,* np.

[76] The indifferent attitude of the government was clear in this regard. H.A.F. Lindsay, Under-Secretary department of Commerce and Industry enquired from the Financial Secretary to the Punjab Government in April 1915 about the measures taken to promote industrial enterprize in the province. The Financial Secretary replied in the negative: *Progs. Commerce and Industry (Industries)*, April 1916, 87. Earlier in 1908, the Punjab government had responded to a proposal of the Government of India to prepare detailed reports on the condition of industries by stating that in view of the 'simple nature' of the handicrafts, and the 'small capital employed it did not appear that any thing more than that was required at the moment'. It further stated 'nor would such a survey bring us in any degree nearer to the desired object': *Progs. Commerce and Industry (Industries), July 1908*, 4.

1921.[77] There was an expansion in industries during the 1930s also. In 1940 the number of industrial concerns was about 900.[78] Some of the capital was invested in the manufacture of goods allied to agriculture. These industries involved relatively simple knowledge and skill, and catered to the needs of local markets.[79] On the whole, the Punjab could not be termed as an industrially developed province.

The attitude of the Punjab government in this matter remained ambivalent. No adequate attention appears to have been paid towards the development of industry or to improve the indigenous products.[80] The records of the department of industries Punjab are absolutely clear about this. The correspondence between the secretary to the Government of Punjab and the secretary to the Government of India dated 18 April 1921 stated:

There were no agricultural engineering works of any

[77] Table showing the number of factories and operatives under the Indian Factories Act during 1921-31:

Year	*Factories*	*Operatives*
1921	297	42,428
1922	366	46,588
1923	399	48,110
1924	434	50,842
1925	527	53,533
1926	548	52,648
1927	546	50,088
1928	602	51,613
1929	613	49,875
1930	640	49,549
1931	647	——

Source: *Census Punjab 1931*, pt I, 41.

[78] In 1940, the number of factories in the Punjab was 917: a number of factories were manufacturing sugarcane crushers and oil engines at Batala and Lahore; textile mills were working at Montgomery and Lyallpur; and steel rolling mills had also come into existence: *Census Punjab 1951,* pt I-A, 60-70.

[79] See also, Khanna, 83

[80] *Progs. Department of Commerce and Industry (Indsutries), July 1905,* 11, file No. 24; *ibid., April 1916,* Nos. 1 and 87.

> size....The director of industries has no workshop or laboratory at his disposal... There exists no government organisation for training mechanical engineers or chemists...Regarding cottage industries, the only action taken up to the present is to open five handloom weaving schools. Upto date no industrial society has been initiated by the department of industries. Government has not given any direct financial aid to individuals or companies nor to small or cottage industries.[81]

The amount of effort and money spent for these purposes was rather meagre.[82] The government was not interested, it seems, in the promotion of technical education either. The few government run industrial schools did not attract many pupils for training.[83] The improved handlooms did not find much favour with the weavers because, among other things, they were fearful of the functioning of these looms. Nothing was done to educate the weavers properly to enable them to get rid of their fears.[84]

The system of education introduced by the British eventually enabled the artisans also to benefit from it in order to improve their social position. The Board of Administration initiated the process by which the people of the Punjab were to be equipped for receiving 'the patronage' enjoyed by the 'natives of Hindostan'.[85] The new system of education took

[81] *From the Secretary to Government of Punjab (Transferred Departments) to the Secretary to the Government of India (Department of Industries) No. 12242, C & I, April 1921, Lahore: Summary of the Action Taken on the Recommendations of Indian Industrial Commission.*

[82] Baij Nath, 130-31; Badenoch, 5.

[83] There were some industrial schools. These were the Mayo School of Art and Government Technical School at Lahore; Institute for the Blind and Government Central Weaving Institute at Amritsar; Government Institute of Dyeing and Calico-Printing, Shahdara; Government Hosiery Institute, and a Government Demonstration Weaving Factory at Ludhiana: *Census Punjab 1951*, pt I-A, 69-70.

[84] *Progs. Department of Commerce and Industry (Industries), April 1916*, No. 87; *Report of Indian Industrial Commission 1916-18*, 7.

[85] *Punjab Administration Report 1849-50, 1850-51*, 142-43.

off in 1854 with the establishment of the department of education under a Director of Public Instructions. Around this period there were four schools for training of teachers. Urdu was adopted as the medium of instructions and English was to be taught at the district level schools. The educational institutions founded by the government corresponded to three levels of primary, secondary, and higher education, consisting of middle and high schools and colleges.

By 1867-68 there were more than 1900 educational institutions of the government including the Government College at Lahore and over 700 other 'aided' institutions. The number of students was over 88,000, over 80 per cent of whom were in government institutions.[86] In 1903-04 there were over 2900 primary schools, 269 middle schools and 110 high schools. There were 15 arts and 3 professional colleges. In 1920 the middle schools numbered 7,865, and the number of secondary schools was 454. In 1902, there were only 10 colleges; the number rose to 40 in 1938.[87] In 1921-22 there were 74,000 boys and girls in 'unrecognised' institutions and over 5,50,000 in government institutions.[88] The government encouraged secondary and higher education partly with an eye on its requirements of Urdu knowing administrative personnel at the lower rungs. The knowledge of English was required, however, for higher positions in administration which were very few.[89] An attempt was made to extend education to the countryside as well.

The efforts of the government to spread education were supplemented by those of the Christian missions and other private organizations like the Arya Samajes, the Singh Sabhas and the Muslim Anjumans. The Christian missionary schools played a great role in spreading English education in the province. The Christian missionaries established several stations in all the major administrative centres in the Punjab

[86] *Punjab Administration Report 1867-68,* 89-98.

[87] Surinder Kaur, 72, 81-82, 100-02.

[88] Trevaskis, 142.

[89] Jones (1976), 60.

during the 1850s.[90] The American Presbyterians and Church of England Communion were the first to open schools.[91] The Presbyterians opened a primary school at Lahore in December 1849. By 1901-2 there were 30 such schools in the Punjab. Besides schools the missionaries opened colleges for higher education as well.[92]

The spread of education by Christian missions had the twin objective of spreading the idea of social equality and to attract more and more people to the fold of Christianity. The missionaries denounced the institution of caste and its built-in system of inequalities. This evoked response from the artisans, particularly from amongst the Chamars and Chuhras, who were in the largest number among the low castes in the Punjab and were easily prone to conversion. Their response to Christianity was essentially due to the promise of a better social status.[93]

The conversion of the low-castes to Christianity evoked reaction from the Punjab leaders, particularly the Aryas.[94] The Arya Samajes, the first Samaj having been founded by Swami Dayanand Saraswati in the Punjab in 1877, attempted to modernize Hinduism.[95] They aimed at adapting the Hindu religion to the social, political and cultural needs of contemporary Indian situation. The Dayanand Anglo-Vedic schools and colleges were founded to counter the challenge of the Christian missionaries. The first D.A.V. institution was started in 1886, and by 1920 the samajists had started 26 schools and 2 colleges in over a dozen districts of the Punjab.[96] The D.A.V. movement aimed at spreading the

[90] The first Christian mission was opened in Ludhiana in 1834. It was only after 1849 that its activities were spread in the Punjab: Lohelin, 189.

[91] Jones (1976), 8.

[92] The colleges opened by missionaries were: The Foreman Christian College, Lahore; Murray College, Sialkot; the Edwards College, Peshawar; and the Gordon College, Rawalpindi: Chhabra, 165; Saini, 71.

[93] Webster, 46-92; Jones (1976), 8-12,

[94] Jones (1990), 87.

[95] Jones (1990), 95-102.

[96] The D.A.V. institutions were established at Lahore, Amritsar, Gurdaspur, Jalandhar, Hoshiarpur, Ludhiana, Rawalpindi, Multan, Peshawar,

knowledge of the Vedas, Sanskrit and Western literature.[97]

The Samajes made determined efforts to contain the movement of the lower castes away from Hinduism. Lajpat Rai remarked from the platform of Arya Samaj that the 'possibility of losing untouchables has shaken the intelligent section of Hindu community and made them aware of the condition of these classes'.[98] The Arya Samajists decried social inequalities and encouraged egalitarianism by inter-dining with members of the lower castes and by admitting them to schools.[99] A subsidiary organization was established at Hoshiarpur known as Dayanand Dalit Udhar Mandal, for the social uplift of the lower castes.[100] This was meant to win converts back from Christianity and Sikhism. To re-convert people through *shuddhi* or ritual purification was a well considered programme of the Samajists.[101] The *shuddhi* extended to the lower castes a hope to become an honourable part of the community. The instances of large scale *shuddhi* operations were those of the Rahtias, weavers by profession the Meghs, the fishermen; and the Odes who specialized in the digging of canals.[102]

The Sikhs also felt concerned about the Christian missionaries drawing converts from amongst the Sikhs. They

---

Ambala and Shimla: Jones (1976), 215-16,224-35.

[97] In Dayanand Anglo-Vedic schools at the lower primary level the emphasis was on the teaching of Hindi—reading and writing, arithmatic, Sanskrit and geography. English was introduced at upper-primary level along with arithmatic and geography. From 6th to 10th classes Sanskrit, arithmatic, mathematics, English, history, geography and physical sciences were taught: Jones (1976), 322.

[98] Quoted by Saberwal, 9.

[99] Jones (1976), 202-03 and 203-11.

[100] Dayanand Dalit Udhar Mandal was understood as an organization to keep the lower castes under the domination of the upper castes. Incidentally its president was Devi Chand, a Khatri: See Sharma (1983), 134.

[101] The concept of *shuddhi* involved the restoration of individuals to purity and fellowship of the Hindu society. The ceremony was performed in public by the recitation of *mantras* from the Vedas and performing Hom or Yajna. After this meals were served to all and the reconverts blessed and sanctified: Jones (1976), 129-35;

[102] Jones (1976), 207-8.

were worried also about the Sikh rituals and ceremonies giving way to Brahmanical influences.[103] To withstand these challenges, the community leaders sought to determine the distinct rituals for the Sikhs and to enlighten and educate the Sikh masses in social and religious matters. The early attempts in this direction had taken the form of the Nirankari and Namdhari movements, emerging before the onset of British rule in the Punjab.

The Nirankaris advocated the need of specifically Sikh ceremonies and mode of worship.[104] The Namdharis emphasized the importance of the baptism of the double-edged sword, the idea of equality among the Khalsa, and the need of literacy for religious worship. The protagonists of these movements did not lay stress on secular education, let alone English education.[105] This task was taken up by the Singh Sabhas in the 1880s.

The Singh Sabhas were not only differently oriented but also better organized than the preceding socio-religious reform movements among the Sikhs. The first Singh Sabha was founded at Amritsar in 1873, followed by that of Lahore in 1879. By the end of the nineteenth century, there were more than one hundred Singh Sabhas all over the Punjab.[106]

The major thrust of the Singh Sabhas was to purge Sikhism of non-Sikh elements and social evils, adding or changing elements according to the contemporary requirements. They also aimed at the spread of Sikhism, particularly among the low castes, by offering them social equality, inter-dining and entry into Gurudwaras. They achieved spectacular success in the spread of literacy and modern education.[107]

[103] Khushwant Singh, 136-37.

[104] The message of Baba Dayal was based on the teachings of Guru Nanak. The Nirankaris believe in the 'Nirankar' or the formless God and in the attainment of salvation through his contemplation: Webster (1979), 83-84.

[105] See Fauja Singh, 30-31, 179.

[106] Barrier (1970), xxii.

[107] Gurdarshan Singh, 58.

The Khalsa schools and colleges were the creation of the Singh Sabhas which aimed at educating the Sikh masses so as to enable them to readjust themselves to the changed political, economic and administrative conditions and to compete with other communities in the Punjab for jobs and other opportunities.[108] A significant beginning was made by the establishment of the Khalsa College at Amritsar in 1892. The teaching of Gurmukhi and Sikh scriptures was compulsory at these schools along with the Western learning. From 1908 onwards, the Sikh Education Conference was convened every year to take stock of the progress of literacy in the community. By 1947, the Sikhs had the maximum literacy rate in the Punjab.[109]

The response of the artisan castes to educational opportunities was rather slow. In the beginning of the 1880s, children from 'humble homes in towns and villages' had started going to educational institutions, particularly those run by the reform organizations.[110] Very few boys and girls from the lower castes, however, could proceed beyond the middle school. The majority of parents withdrew their children after the primary level to enable them to work in their family occupations.[111] By the end of the nineteenth century, however, some artisans had begun to send their children to high schools to make them eligible for employment in government offices. Data on literacy among the artisans according to the census reports is given in Table I.

As is evident from the table, in 1891 the Sunars formed the largest group among the literate artisans with more than 11,000 persons, followed by 8,000 literates of the Tarkhan caste. Among other castes, the number was much smaller. Within the next 40 years, more of the Tarkhans, Julahas, Sunars, Lohars and the Mochis showed inclination towards receiving education. In terms of absolute numbers the

108 See Khushwant Singh, 142-45 and Barrier (1970), i-xx.

109 Khushwant Singh, 146; Marenco, 97-105.

110 Tandan, 192.

111 Saini, 171-72.

TABLE I

Caste	*1891*	*1911*	*1921*	*1931*	*Per cent increase*
Chamar	4,709	4,219	5,425	6,182	+31.28
Julaha	4,052	5,029	7,218	10,035	+142.65
Kumhar	2,052	2,434	2,854	6,024	+194.34
Lohar	3,391	4,572	4,503	7,909	+133.24
Mochi	1,349	1,426	2,461	4,362	+133.24
Sunar	11,319	12,610	8,270	14,273	+31.84
Tarkhan	8,345	14,808	14,200	21,944	+162.96
Total	35,217	45,098	44,930	70,729	+100.83

maximum increase in literacy was shown by the Tarkhan caste from over 8,000 in 1891 to about 21,000 in 1931. They were followed by the Sunars and the Julahas. The proportion of literate artisans to the total literates in the Punjab, however, did not appreciably change. The literate artisans formed a little more than 5 per cent of the total from 1891 to 1931. However, the number of literate artisans rose from 35,000 in 1891 to more than 70,000 in 1931—a hundred per cent increase. Correspondingly the total literate population of the Punjab as a whole increased from merely 6.7 lacs in 1891 to 12.6 lacs in 1931—an increase of 87 per cent.[112]

The spread of literacy as well as the developments in the economic life in the Punjab under colonial rule offered new opportunities to the artisan castes. Socio-religious reform movements and educational institutions equipped the artisans to take up new occupations and enabled them to improve their social and economic position in a significant manner.

[112]

Census	*Total literate population of the Punjab*	*Proportion of the literates among the artisan castes*
1891	6,75,941	5.21
1911	7,74,845	5.82
1921	8,85,837	5.07
1931	12,65,401	5.09

Source: Based on the census reports of 1891, 1921 and 1931.

CHAPTER FIVE

Towards New Occupations

Occupational mobility was a general phenomenon under British rule. By 1931 about 25 per cent of all castes had abandoned their hereditary occupations; another 25 per cent had adopted other occupations as their principal means of livelihood while retaining the traditional one as subsidiary occupation.[1] In the Punjab too similar tendencies are in evidence. By 1911, for example, 67 per cent of the total working Chamars were not engaged in their traditional occupation; the proportion of the Kumhars who had abandoned their profession was 48 per cent; while among the Tarkhans the percentage was 42; among the Lohars 45; and it was 36 among the Mochis; 32 per cent of the Julahas had moved away from their hereditary occupation and the percentage was 16 among the Sunars.[2] The tendency was accelerated and by 1931, 90 per cent of the Kumhars and 76 per cent of the Chamars were not engaged in their traditional occupations.[3] The pattern of mobility, to begin with, was more in the form of positional change. The movement in positional change implied a shift to the next higher evaluated occupation without causing any serious disruption in the hierarchy of caste and occupations.[4] For example, the Chamars who took

[1] Among the Chamars the proportion of those who abandoned their hereditary occupation was much greater; twelve out of thirteen Chamars had stopped working in leather as their principal means of livelihood: *Census India 1931*, Vol I, pt I, 296.

[2] The percentages have been worked out on the basis of the number of actual workers: *Census Punjab 1911*, pt II, 424-35.

[3] *Census Punjab 1931*, pt II, 220, 222.

[4] Ibbetson, 266-67.

to weaving as a profession, signified this change. The Julaha as a caste and as an occupation was placed immediately next higher to the Chamar and leather work. With the passage of time, and because of the increasing educational and economic opportunities caste barriers began to be transcended in search of new occupations.

II

In the initial stages acquisition of land and turning to agriculture was the most obvious recourse taken by the artisans. As already pointed out, the occupational pattern in villages in the Punjab centred round land and so was the social hierarchy. The ownership of land was acknowledged as the source of political power and social prestige.[5] The landowners in the Punjab, therefore, considered themselves as the highest caste, and regarded all others, including the Brahmans, as lower to themselves.[6] In the absence of any other opportunity taking to agriculture as a profession could, therefore, be a channel for the artisans to raise themselves in social hierarchy, both within their own caste group and in inter-caste relationships. Those artisans who had saved money tended to invest it in land. The keenness to adopt agriculture as their profession by the artisans such as the Tarkhans, Lohars and the Chamars has been noticed by several settlement officers during the first half of the colonial period.

The Tarkhans and Lohars had become the hereditary owners of land even before the beginning of British rule in the Punjab.[7] In the early 1880s, they cultivated over 7,000 acres

[5] Ibbetson, 215. See also Srinivas, 13.

[6] It may be added that on this particular question, the respondents of the artisan castes also emphatically stated that the Jats did not acknowledge any other caste as equal to themselves.

[7] See for example, *SR Panipat and Karnal 1872-80,* Lii-Liv; *SR Jalandhar 1880-84*, Appendix I, cxiv; *SR Rohtak 1873-79,* Table IX; *SR Gurdaspur 1859,* 44-45.

Some Tarkhans in the paraganas of Pathankot, Gurdaspur and Batala were holding land as owners.

of land in Jalandhar district and also held several villages in hereditary ownership.[8] Apart from owning land themselves, the Lohars shared some villages with Tarkhans and one village with the Nais in Jalandhar. In the Nakodar tahsil of Jalandhar district, they owned a village named Lohar-Nangal; they owned one-fourth of village named Pindori near Jandiala in Phillaur tahsil; they had some shares in another village named Gurkha as well.[9] In Karnal district in eastern Punjab, 165 Lohars were non-cultivating proprietors in the 1870s.[10] In Ludhiana district, the Tarkhans owned shares in several villages.[11] Even in the far off district of Dera Ghazi Khan in western Punjab, the Lohars and the Tarkhans owned respectively 2,667 and 6,309 acres of land.[12]

In 1891, the number of Lohars and Tarkhans as agriculturists was the largest among the artisan castes. At this time, 23.95 per cent of the actual workers among the Tarkhans were engaged in agriculture and this percentage was 16.27 among the Lohars.[13] Within two decades, the percentage of the actual workers among the Tarkhans who were enumerated as agriculturists rose to 28.47; it was nearly doubled in case of the Lohars, touching 28.75 per cent.[14] The Tarkhans, however, constituted the largest group as the non-cultivating proprietors with 5,080 persons, followed by 1,515 persons of the Lohar caste.[15]

[8] *SR Jalandhar 1880-84*, Appendix I. See also Dungen (1968), 64.

[9] *SR Jalandhar 1880-84*, Appendix I.

[10] *DG Jalandhar 1904*, 104.

[11] *SR Ludhiana 1878-83*, 53.

[12] *SR Dera Ghazi Khan 1869-74*, Appendix V.

[13] Among the Tarkhans 8,246 persons were non-cultivating proprietors while 14,235 persons were owner-cultivators and 32,933 were cultivating land as tenants. The number of non-cultivating proprietors among the Lohars was 1,055; 7,128 persons were owner-cultivators and 15,421 were registered as.tenants: *Census Punjab 1891*, pt II, 552-60.

[14] The total number of the actual workers among the Tarkhans was 2,29,433 out of which 65,378 were agriculturists: *Census Punjab 1911*, pt II, 428-29, 432-33.

[15] The number of Lohar cultivators, including tenants, was 27,239 and field- labourers among them were 3,663. Among the Tarkhans, 54,947 were

The number of the Chamars pursuing agriculture as their profession in 1891 was 42,640 out of whom 1,223 were non-cultivating proprietors while 14,933 were recorded as owner-cultivators and more than 25,000 as tenants.[16] By 1911, however, more than 39 per cent of the Chamars had adopted agriculture as their principal means of livelihood. Thus, by this time in the Punjab, more than 1.84 lacs Chamars were the owner-cultivators or field labourers and 1,742 persons among them were non-cultivating proprietors.[17]

The Julahas were the other important caste to take up agriculture in large numbers. There were more than 50,000 Julahas cultivating land in 1891.[18] The percentage of the Julahas pursuing agriculture as their main profession was 14.15 in 1911 out of whom 74.23 per cent were owner-cultivators and 22.15 per cent were field labourers, and only 3.60 per cent returned themselves as non-cultivating proprietors.[19]

The Kumhars adopted agriculture as their means of earning livelihood rather late. The early references suggesting their movement towards agriculture are very few. For instance, in 1872-80, there were 206 Kumhars engaged in agriculture in Panipat and Karnal Parganas but most of them were either tenants or field labourers and in Gohana tahsil they owned only 29 acres of land.[20] In 1891, in the Punjab as a whole,

---

returned as cultivators and 4,876 as field labourers: *Census Punjab 1911*, pt II, 429, 433.

[16] *Census Punjab 1891*, pt II, 558-60.

[17] The number of cultivators among the Chamars was 90,367 and those of field labourers 92,464: *Census Punjab 1911*, pt II, 424-25.

[18] The number of non-cultivating proprietors among them was 2,263; 9,518 were owner-cultivators and 38,685 were enumerated as tenants: *Census Punjab 1891*, pt II, 552-60.

[19] The absolute number of the agriculturist Julahas in 1911 had declined due to the exclusion of the areas of Delhi and North Western Frontier Province from the Punjab. The number of non-cultivating proprietors was 1,372 and those of the owner-cultivators 28,226. There were now 8,423 Julahas as field labourers: *Census Punjab 1911*, pt II, 429.

[20] *SR Panipat and Karnal 1872-80*, liv; *SR Rohtak 1873-79*, np.

6.42 per cent of the Kumhars were engaged in agriculture.[21] By 1911, the proportion of agriculturists among them, however, rose to 20.81 per cent.[22]

The Mochis also showed some interest in land. The earlier instances of acquisition of land by them are available from the district of Dera Ghazi Khan where by the end of the 1860s they held about 4,600 acres of land.[23] In 1891, 8.10 per cent of the Mochis were enumerated as agriculturists in the Punjab. Of these 34.79 per cent were owner-cultivators, 59 per cent cultivated land as tenants, and 2.48 per cent were returned as non-cultivating proprietors.[24] In 1911, about 18 per cent of the Mochis were enumerated as agriculturists. Of them, 11.43 per cent were cultivators of all kinds, and 7.38 per cent were either farm-labourers or non-cultivating proprietors.[25]

The Sunars were an exception to the trend among the artisans in their movement towards agriculture. In the returns of 1891, 5,608 Sunars or 2.85 per cent of the total caste were shown as agriculturists, out of whom 1,688 were owner-cultivators and 113 non-cultivating proprietors.[26] Some isolated examples of the Sunars as agriculturists can also be cited, as for example, in the areas covered by the former parganas of Panipat and Karnal, where 103 persons of the Sunar caste were cultivating land with 22 out of them as proprietors.[27] In Dera

[21] The number of owner-cultivators among the Kumhars was 2,970 and those of non-cultivating proprietors was 282: *Census Punjab 1891*, pt II, 552-60.

[22] The number of owner-cultivators among the Kumhars was 34,985 and 5,461 were field labourers; the non-cultivating proprietors were 1,582 in number: *Census Punjab 1911*, pt II, 428-29.

[23] *SR Dera Ghazi Khan 1869-79*, cxiv.

[24] In all 42,640 of the Mochis were agriculturists of which 14,836 were owner-cultivators, 25,176 tenants and 1,060 were non-cultivating proprietors: *Census Punjab 1891*, pt II, 552-60.

[25] In 1911, the non-cultivating proprietors among the Mochis were 1,386; 4,850 worked as the farm servants; 17,050 were the owner-cultivators, and 180 were the agents of landed estates: *Census Punjab 1911*, pt II, 428-29.

[26] *Census Punjab 1891*, pt II, 552-60.

[27] *SR Panipat and Karnal 1872-80*, liv.

Ghazi Khan district, the Sunars owned 2,492 acres of land, in all probability as non-cultivating proprietors.[28]

The census reports of 1921 and 1931 indicate that a good proportion among the artisans continued as agriculturists. In 1921, for instance, there were 30,064 owner-cultivators of the Tarkhan caste, although the number of those returned as field labourers was reported to be rather small.[29] In 1931, however, more than 48,000 Tarkhans, that is about 22 per cent of those engaged in gainful economic activity, had been enumerated as agriculturists in different capacities.[30] Similarly in 1921 more than 1,66,000 and in 1931 more than 1,63,000 of the Chamars were returned as agriculturists.[31] In 1931, 13.42 per cent among the Lohars were agriculturists, and among them 14.60 per cent were owner-cultivators.[32] In case of the Kumhars the proportion of those engaged in agriculture was 22.17 per cent of which 53 per cent were owner-cultivators.[33]

[28] *SR Dera Ghazi Khan 1869-74*, lxiv.

In Rohtak tahsil, the Sunars held 57 acres of land: *SR Rohtak 1873-79*, Table IX.

[29] The number of field-labourers among Tarkhans is stated to be just 1,626 which does not seem to be correct: *Census Punjab 1921*, pt II, 384-85.

[30] The total number of actual workers of the Tarkhans was 2,21,494 out of which 48,125 were agriculturists and 65.23 per cent of them were the owner-cultivators: *Census Punjab 1931*, pt II, 220-22.

[31] In 1921 the number of actual workers among the Chamars was 4,10,515 out of which 1,66,700 were agriculturists and 50 per cent among them were owner-cultivators. In 1931, the proportion of the agriculturists among the Chamars actually engaged in gainful economic activity was 40 per cent: *Census Punjab 1921*, pt II, 380-91; *Census Punjab 1931*, pt II, 221-22.

[32] The data for the Lohars is relevant for the districts of eastern Punjab, central Punjab plains and central Punjab hills and cover partly the areas of western Punjab. Also, these figures relate to Hindu and Sikh Lohars alone. The census returns do not include Muslims, probably because occupational mobility among them was relatively small. The actual workers were 1,74,219 and among them 24,211 were agriculturists in different capacities. 1,180 Lohars were non-cultivating proprietors and 14,625 were returned as the owner-cultivators. The number of field labourers among them was rather small: *Census Punjab 1931*, pt II, 221-23.

[33] The data for the Kumhars is relevant for the districts of the eastern

It is relevant to point out that the number of those among the artisan castes engaged in agriculture in different capacities did not increase during the period between 1911 and 1931. The number of those engaged in agriculture in 1911 was more than 3.11 lacs which decreased to 3.9 lacs in 1921 and further to 2.9 lacs in 1931.[34] The movement of artisans towards agriculture, particularly as owners was restricted by the provisions of the Alienation of Land Act 1900 which did not include them as 'agriculturists' and they were, therefore, not entitled to purchase agricultural land or get it on mortgage.[35] Those who held land and were not notified as agriculturists felt their exclusion as a disqualification and a hurdle in their quest for higher social status. The Tarkhans even filed a petition pleading their case for inclusion among agricultural castes, but in vain.[36] The process of acquisition of land by the artisan castes was thus hampered.[37]

III

The ineligibility forced by the Alienation of Land Act obliged the artisans to explore other available avenues of employment requiring their traditional skills. Many of them migrated to work as independent workers in urban areas of Amritsar, Lahore, Sialkot, Hoshiarpur and Jalandhar to work at new

---

Punjab, central Punjab hills and central Punjab plains and for Hindus and Sikhs only. Actual workers among them were 73,306, and out of them 15,488 persons were engaged in agriculture. The number of owner-cultivators was 12,389 and those of non-cultivating proprietors was only 231: *Census Punjab 1931*, pt II, 221-23.

[34] Data calculated on the basis of: *Census Punjab 1911*, pt II, 424-32; *Census Punjab 1921*, pt II, 380-87; *Census Punjab 1931*, pt II, 220,227.

[35] The Act of 1900 notified the Jat, Arain, Awan and Rajput as agricultural castes. It was designed mainly to prevent the acquisition of land by money-lenders from amongst the trading castes: Barrier (1979), 213-15.

[36] Dungen (1972), 283-85.

[37] According to the Punjab Land Administration Manual, the members of artisan castes who were not money-lenders could purchase land for agricultural purposes only when it was established that it was not disadvantageous to the seller and his family: quoted in Nihal Chand Anand, 183.

constructions. A good number of them joined factories in different capacities. Some of the small scale units were owned by the artisans themselves. A small number of the artisan castes took to trade and a small proportion of the educated among them joined various public services. But on the whole jobs requiring little or no education were more important. Till 1911, a large proportion of those engaged in industries worked mostly as labourers or as skilled workers. As indicated in the following table the number of owners, managers and clerks among them remained rather small.[38]

TABLE I

Caste	*Owners, Managers and clerks*	*Labourers and skilled workers*
Chamar	2,526	71,241
Mochi	296	16,463
Kumhar	500	11,091
Julaha	292	10,835
Lohar	266	7,490
Tarkhan	627	1,527
Sunar	52	1,933
Total	4,559	1,20,580

In 1911 as the table shows the Chamars were largest in number, in both the white collar and skilled jobs in factory industries, accounting for 15 per cent of the Chamars engaged in gainful economic activity. The Tarkhans were the second largest caste to be the owners and managers, with 11 per cent of the total followed by the Kumhars with more than 5 per cent of the caste. They were followed by the Mochis, Julahas and the Lohars. The number of Sunars both as workers and owners was very small. Apparently, there was no great movement among the Sunars towards industries.[39]

[38] *Census Punjab 1911*, pt I, 502; pt II, 424-25, 429, 433.

[39] Percentage of the actual workers engaged in gainful economic activity in industry in different capacities among the artisans in 1911 was as follows:

The specific evidence available for the later period also points to this trend. In 1921, for instance, there were 943 Chamars, 2,418 Lohars and 1,620 Tarkhans working in some of the fairly large cotton ginning and pressing, spinning and weaving mills, woollen mills, carpet factories, leather dyeing factories, tea processing factories and salt mines. Most of them were engineers, fitters and mechanics, oilmen or engine drivers, carpenters, packers and despatchers.[40] The total number of workmen from among the artisan castes, including unskilled labourers, was however, 47,016 Chamars, 6,484 Kumhars and 10,818 Mochis.[41]

In the railway worshops in the Punjab in 1923, there were enumerated 1,272 Tarkhans, 2,012 Lohars and 147 Chamars as workmen. These three castes together formed 31 per cent of total persons working in the railway workshops.[42]

In 1931, the number of Chamars working in skilled jobs and as labourers in different industries was 38,878 followed by 9,782 persons of the Mochi caste. The number of persons from other castes, however, was small: the number of Tarkhans was about 5,600 and the Julahas were 6,350. The number of the Sunars in both the categories was the minimum: respectively 44 and 1,089 only.[43]

The artisans as skilled workers in factories were earning fairly well. In 1906, the skilled blacksmiths and carpenters earned between 15 and 30 rupees a month. In 1912 the range

Cast	*Per cent of the total*	*Caste*	*Per cent of the total*
Chamar	15.63	Lohar	6.83
Mochi	11.23	Tarkhan	.93
Kumhar	5.72	Sunar	3.66

Source: *Census Punjab 1911*, pt II, 424-25, 429, 433.

[40] *Census Punjab 1921*, pt II, Table on 'Caste or Race of Skilled Workmen Classified according to Industry and Occupation'.

[41] *Census Punjab 1921*, pt II, 380-84.

[42] *Progs. Department of Industries and Labour (Labour), L 812 (6) of 1923: Industrial Statistics*, 418-419. There were nine railway workshops in the Punjab in 1925: *Progs.Industries and Labour (Factories), L 1516 of 1928.*

[43] *Census Punjab 1931*, pt II, 223, 224, 225.

of monthly wages for blacksmiths and carpenters was between 17 and 26 rupees. During and after World War I the increase in their wages was substantial: the upper range reached 40 rupees a month in 1917, 46 in 1928 and 54 rupees in 1932. The following table indicating wages of carpenters and blacksmiths working in factories at different points of time in Amritsar, Lahore and Gurdaspur districts explains further.[44]

TABLE II: RANGE OF WAGES
(in rupees per month)

Year	*Blacksmiths*	*Carpenters*
1906	17-24	15-30
1912	17-22	11.5-24
1916-17	15-40	20-40
1922-28	40-44	40-46
1932	30-54	52.5–

The wages of the qualified engineers were still higher. In 1915 a first class engineer earned a salary between 70 and 130 rupees a month in the Punjab. The second class engineers earned between 60 and 100 rupees a month.[45] In 1929 a qualified engineer was paid at the rate of 75 rupees in Ludhiana and 100 rupees in Jalandhar and Lyallpur.[46] Even the unskilled artisans had better opportunities to earn more in urban areas.[47]

The reputation and remuneration the artisans earned while working in the Punjab helped them to find their way to distant places in the country and abroad. The British found the Punjabi artisans more efficient, skilled and enterprizing than

[44] Data adapted from: *Progs. Commerce and Industry (Factories), October 1907*, 7; *ibid., December 1908*, 2; *ibid., November 1910*, 1-13A; *ibid., November 1912*, 1-14; *ibid., June 1916*, 1-23/A; *ibid., May 1917*, 1-19A; *Progs. Industries and Labour (Factories), L-1516 (1) of 1928; Progs. Industries and Labour (Labour-A), 25A, 1932.*

[45] *Progs. Commerce and Industry (Factories-A), June 1916*, 1-23A.

[46] *Progs. Industries and Labour (Labour-A), 25A, 1932.*

[47] *Fifth Regular Wages Survey*, 3.

their counterparts elsewhere in the country.[48] Their products were also recommended for export to European markets.[49] Their energies and skills were harnessed also to new purposes like making high quality furniture, cutlery and fine metal works for the British clientele.[50] Badenoch describes the quality of cutlery produced at Wazirabad and Nizamabad as 'good and expensive'.[51] Some Tarkhans were sent to Kensington School of Art, London to train in new techniques.[52]

The quality of the work of the Punjabi Lohars and Tarkhans induced the British administrators to recommend them to work in the areas where local skills were inadequate. The enterprizing Tarkhans and Lohars, in fact, were the first ones to avail of opportunities available outside the Punjab. They went as far as to Assam to work on the laying down of the railway track under difficult conditions. From village Gaggar Bhana in Amritsar district out of twenty two families of Tarkhans seventeen families, consisting of eighty four persons, went to distant areas for service, while twenty four out of them worked at the railway workshop at Amritsar. The Mochis from the same village moved as far as to Bengal and Bihar to work in coal mines.[53] Large scale construction works in Shimla, the summer capital, and in New Delhi the new capital, besides the canal colony areas, provided the Lohars and Tarkhans with good opportunities of gainful employment.[54]

The artisans were also called upon to work in various British colonies in Africa and Latin America.[55] They were doing both

48 Saberwal (1977), 102.

49 The monograph on wood manufactures stated 'there was no reason why the Punjab wood work, which was at the same time portable, should not find a ready market in Europe': *Monograph on Wood Manufactures*, 5-6.

50 See Baden-Powell, 249-50.

51 Badenoch, 34.

52 *Monograph on Wood Manufactures*, 6. The actual number of those sent to the Kensington School of Art is not indicated.

53 *Economic Survey of Gaggar Bhana*, 19-20.

54 Saberwal (1977), 160-61.

55 *Progs. Commerce and Industry (Emigration)-A, file No. 13-16 of*

skilled and unskilled work in laying down the railway track and also in the building of the rolling stock in British East Africa and Uganda.[56] The Punjabi artisans who migrated to British East Africa made good fortunes from the construction work for the government and private owners. A first class mason and carpenter earned between 50 and 100 rupees per month.[57] As a result, a large number of Punjabi artisans were attracted towards working in Africa even in contravention of the contracts made by them with government agencies at the time of emigration.[58] A considerable number of Punjabi artisans also found their way to Brazil, Argentina, Cuba and to the United States of America.[59] Other areas of their adventure were New Zealand, Fiji, Trinidad, Jamaica, Guiana, Malay Straits and Hong Kong. Those who migrated were generally from among the skilled artisans and usually Sikhs from the central Punjab. They were attracted by the spirit of adventure combined with the high wages they expected to receive as policemen, watchmen, miners and contractors.[60] From the village Phalpota in Jalandhar district, 2 per cent Chamars and

---

1906. The government permitted the Indian families to settle in British East Africa.

56 About 12,000 Indians among whom the Punjabi artisans were in large number migrated to Uganda in 1908 to work on Ugandan Railways: *Progs. Commerce and Industry (Emigration),1908*, file no. 66.

57 *Progs. Commerce and Industry (Emigration), April 1912*, 19-24. The private building contractors paid more than the government agencies.

58 Under the emigration rules, the artisans were supposed to work under government contractors till the completion of their projects. If they contravened in this rule, they were deprived of the benefit of free passage back to India. The artisans would often break themselves away from their contract by paying nominal penalty and foregoing their free passage so that they could earn much more by working for private contractors: *Progs. Commerce and Industry (Emigration)-A ,1910*, 1-2; *ibid., 1912*, 42.

59 *Progs. Commerce and Industry (Emigration), May 1912*, 1-6; *ibid.,1914*, 7-15.

60 In 1911, 809 artisans from central Punjab went to Fiji, 7,574 to Federated Malay straits, 1,197 to Hong Kong and 985 to Strait Settlements. Their number was large enough to pose problems for the emigration departments of Fiji, Jamaica, Trinidad and Guiana: *Progs. Commerce and Industry (Emigration)*-A, 1917, 76-41.

1 per cent of the Julahas had migrated to other countries by 1898, and in 1910, the proportion of the Chamars migrating to other countries was 1 per cent and those of the Julahas 3 per cent. By 1922, 9 per cent Julahas had migrated to other countries.[61] From the districts of Hoshiarpur and Jalandhar, about 12 per cent of the emigrants to New Zealand during 1912-1939 were the Chamars.[62]

Petty trading seemed to be an avenue for those artisans who had been pushed out of their traditional occupations, but could not be absorbed by the limited expansion of factories and other opportunities requiring their hereditary skills. Initially, the Kumhars dealt mainly in grain and earned their livelihood as carriers of goods between villages and towns. The Kumhars had, in fact, been traditionally engaged in local trade, using their donkeys and mules for this purpose. They dealt chiefly in *gur* and grain.[63] The Julahas were rather simple traders and we do not get any impression that they moved about much with their goods. They were working mostly as petty shopkeepers where they would sell vegetables, fruit and tobacco.[64] In the census of 1911, 5,725 Kumhars and 2,578 Julahas returned themselves as engaged in trade. Over 1,300 Mochis and 1,500 Chamars were also shown among traders.[65] In 1921 also, the number of Kumhar traders was larger than those among the Julahas. The proportion of the Kumhars engaged in trade was 32 per thousand. Among other castes, the number of traders was rather small except the Sunars, among whom 18 per thousand were engaged in trade.[66] The table III explains further.

[61] See Kessinger, 166.

[62] The total number of the migrants was 302 and the Chamars numbered 39 among them. They were the second largest group after the Jats whose number was 132: Mcleod, 76-77.

[63] *Village Survey Gaggar Bhana*, 13.

[64] *Village Survey Gaggar Bhana*, 25.

[65] *Census Punjab 1911*, pt I, 426, 430, 434.

[66] *Census Punjab 1921*, pt I, 389; pt II, 380-87.

TABLE III: THE ARTISANS CASTES ENGAGED IN TRADE IN 1911 AND 1921

Caste	Total Persons engaged in Trade 1911	1921
Kumhar	5,725	5,974
Chamar	1,576	3.034
Julaha	2,578	2,803
Mochi	541	1,194
Tarkhan	909	529
Sunar	787	543

The educated among the artisan castes went in for government services. Some of them even became commissioned and gazetted officers in the army and the police, and could also be found in civil administration as gazetted officers. In 1911, 86 commissioned officers in army and police were from among the artisan castes and 2,785 persons were enumerated as belonging to 'other' professions. In civil administration 62 gazetted officers were from among the artisan castes. The total number of the artisan castes in government services was nearly 5,000 and more than 1,200

TABLE IV: DETAILS OF COMMISSIONED AND GAZETTED OFFICERS, LAWYERS DOCTORS AND TEACHERS

Caste	Public Forces: Commiss-ioned officers	Public Forces: Others	Administration: Gazetted Officers	Administration: Others	Lawyers/Doctors Teachers and other Professions
Chamar	11	589	2	577	147
Julaha	3	965	4	1,117	432
Kumhar	8	293	13	304	119
Lohar	17	174	11	289	106
Mochi	14	364	7	407	129
Sunar	6	80	10	1,700	101
Tarkhan	27	320	15	576	175
Total	86	2,785	62	4,970	1,209

persons were returned as lawyers, doctors and teachers.[67] The following table explains further.

By 1921, the number of commissioned officers from among the artisan castes in the public forces increased from 86 to 92 and those of the gazetted officers from 62 to 89.[68] The following table elaborates further.

TABLE V

Caste	*Commissioned Officers*	*Gazetted Officers*
Chamar	5	13
Julaha	26	18
Kumhar	13	3
Lohar	16	27
Mochi	2	10
Sunar	23	4
Tarkhan	7	14
Total	92	89

In 1931, however, the commissioned and gazetted officers in civil administration and armed forces from among the artisan castes were returned in smaller numbers: 53 and 29 respectively.[69] The number of lawyers, doctors and teachers, nevertheless registered an increase during 1921-1931 as following comparative table shows.

TABLE VI

Caste	*Number of Lawyers, Doctors and Teachers*	
	1921	*1931*
Chamar	79	130
Julaha	504	748
Kumhar	160	86
Lohar	110	182
Mochi	120	247
Sunar	94	212
Tarkhan	132	409
Total	1,199	2,014

67 *Census Punjab 1911*, pt II, 426, 427, 430-31.

68 *Census Punjab 1921*, pt II, 380-84.

69 *Census Punjab 1931*, pt II, 227.

In 1921, 1,199 artisans figured in this category. Nearly 50 per cent of whom were the Julahas, followed by the Kumhars, Tarkhans, Lohars and others. This number increased to 2,014 in 1931, with the Julahas and Tarkhans forming a significant proportion among them.[70]

IV

The movement to change occupations among artisans, however, was not very considerable as can be seen from the above discussion. The artisans were slow to respond to the combined effect of the various developments like colonization, extension of cultivation, commercialization of agriculture, development of industry, the means of communications and the spread of literacy. The process of change was gradual and complex. At the same time, however, the view of the census superintendent of the Punjab for 1931 that 'artisans and menials do not find any better substitute for their work to entice them away from their home', can not be accepted.[71] In fact, even in the late nineteenth century, while referring to the movement of the people towards new and higher evaluated occupations, Ibbetson noticed that the 'changes of this sort' however slow, were 'actually in progress' and that 'each caste threw out off-shoots into grades above that were occupied by the greater number of its members'.[72]

By the beginning of the 20th century, a 'striking feature' of the time was the great mobility of labourers 'moving freely' to places where they obtained more remunerative employment.[73] At any rate, by 1931, we know that the proportion of the workers of all castes following traditional occupations had significantly fallen as a result of which the traditional socio-economic set up under *sepi* system had given

[70] *Census Punjab 1921*, pt II, 380-85; *Census Punjab 1931*, pt II, 225, 227.

[71] *Census Punjab 1931*, pt I, 119.

[72] Ibbetson, 267.

[73] *Census Punjab 1911*, pt I, 50.

away, compelling the artisans to look for other avenues of employment. The Chamar, Julaha, Tarkhan, Lohar, and the Kumhar castes were prominent in abandoning their traditional occupations. The tendency to discard traditional occupations was, in fact, more prominent among Hindu and Sikh artisans than Muslims.

The percentage of those who continued to be engaged in their traditional occupations was the largest among the Muslims. The census superintendent of Punjab for 1931 observed that the proportions of workers of each and every caste following occupations had fallen and the castes most conspicuous in discarding their traditional occupations were the Chamars, both Hindus and Sikhs, Hindu Julahas, Hindu Tarkhans and Hindu Lohars.[74] Among Muslim Julahas 78.1 per cent; among Hindus 13.9 per cent and among Sikhs 37.6 per cent were engaged in traditional occupation of the caste. Among Tarkhans and Lohars 41 per cent of Hindus, 56 per cent of Sikhs and 66 per cent Muslim workers followed traditional occupation as against 58, 61 and 72 per cent respectively in 1921.[75] Among Kumhars 13.2 per cent of Hindus, 8.2 per cent of Sikhs and 16.5 per cent of Muslims were engaged in traditional occupation of pottery.[76]

The phenomenon can, perhaps, be explained partly in terms of the slow growth of mechanized industry and partly of the inability on the part of the artisans to respond to new opportunities at a faster pace. The latter may be attributed to the lack of organization, and more particularly, of consciousness among the artisans becuase of which they could not successfully get out of the rut of social disabilities imposed on them for centuries together. Even those who responded to the evangelical appeal of Christianity, Sikhism, Islam and Arya Samaj and changed their religion, soon found to their dismay that the change of religion did not necessarily raise their status. The interviews with the artisan families reveal

[74] *Census Punjab 1931*, pt I, 232.
[75] *Ibid.,* 343.
[76] *Ibid.,* 346.

that most of the tensions in the new social relations were caused by the caste background of the professionally and economically mobile artisans. The new pattern of social relations, therefore, took a long time to correspond to the changed occupations and economic condition.

CHAPTER SIX

New Social Relations

The occupational mobility among the artisan castes changed their roles and social relations.[1] The mobile individuals and groups among them acquired a social and economic position hitherto not enjoyed by their fellow castemen. This brought them face to face with new situations in their social relationships with other castes as well as with the parent castes. To evaluate the experiences of the mobile artisans, a number of individuals of different castes belonging to the districts of Amritsar, Jalandhar, Hoshiarpur, Gujrat, Gujranwala, Montgomery and Lyallpur were interviewed.[2] They were put questions on their experiences with reference to their occupational and economic standing, patterns of social relations, particularly in relation to the land-owners in villages and the upper castes in urban areas.[3]

[1] Each individual occupies or performs a social role. The status acquired by virtue of the nature of role is the collection of rights and duties and to put them into effect in a patterned sequence of action by an individual in an inter-action situation is to perform a role: *A Dictionary of Social Sciences*, 609. See also Yadav, 34.

[2] The respondents referred to as belonging to the districts of Montgomery, Lyallpur, Gujranwala and Gujrat had migrated to the Indian side in 1947.

The respondents were selected at random. A random sample is the one drawn from a single whole on the assumption that each has equal probability of imparting information: Haqood and Price, 272-94. See also Foddy, 189-92.

[3] The interviews with the people of the artisan castes focussed on the subjective experiences, attitudes and responses regarding the situation under study with the help of structured questions. For the nature and definition of focussed interview and structured questionnaire see Young, 218-19.

The upwardly mobile individuals and groups tried to achieve a higher social status for themselves by emulating the customs, manners and eating habits of the groups traditionally superior to themselves.[4] It could be the Jat, the highest evaluated in the village or the immediately next higher caste group as for example, Julaha was the ideal of Chamars. In the process of adopting the behaviour and life style typical of the target groups, the mobile persons tended to dissociate themselves from the parent group in social, economic and cultural terms. Their success, however, depended on the response of the target group.[5] The attitude of the upper castes was generally repelling and they tried to discourage the movement of the lower castes into their occupational sanctuary. This was true particularly of the landowning castes in villages who expressed their indignation over the upward mobility of the *kamins* of yester years in various ways.

II

Under the traditional socio-economic set up comprehended by the *sepi* system the artisans in rural areas lived separately from the upper castes in separate localities or in small exclusive clusters of houses. The residences of the Lohars, Tarkhans, Sunars and the Julahas were generally within the precincts of the village and the untouchables like the Chamars lived at some distance from the village. In larger villages there were different localities for different caste groups and were known by the caste and occupation of the concerned group. For instance, in village Sathiala in Amritsar district, there were separate *mohallas* of the blacksmiths and carpenters as of other castes, known by the name of Loharan-di-Gali, Tarkhana-di-Gali, Brahmana-di-Gali and Khatriyan-di-Gali.[6]

See also Questionnaire in the appendix.

[4] It is possible to apply the 'Sanskritization' model to this situation. 'Sanskritization' implies the adoption of customs, rites, and beliefs of higher evaluated castes. See Srinivas (1970), 2.

[5] See Triandis, 127.

[6] Sathiala is a large village situated 28 kilometers from Amritsar on the

The residential enclosures of the Chamars were called the *thathi* or the *chamarhli.*[7] In all probability, where the number of Chuhras was large, their residential area was known as the *thathi* and those with Chamar dominance were called *chamarhli.*

The *chamarhli* or the *thathi* was situated on the outskirts of the village or about half a kilometer away from the main village site.[8] In village Sohiyan, about eight kilometers away from Amritsar, we even found Kumhars and Tarkhans in the *thathi* living together with the Mazhbis or the Sikh Chuhras and the Jhiwars or the water carriers. In Vilyatpur in Jalandhar district, the leather-workers, and scavengers and weavers lived in separate areas termed as *abadis*. Their houses were separated from the houses of the Jat land-owners by the houses of the potters and dyers who belonged to the 'clean' category among artisans. The houses of the weavers in Vilyatpur were close to the houses of the Chamars and Chuhras.[9] However, we do not find this practice in the villages of Amritsar district where the weavers resided in the neighbourhood of the higher castes. In village Sathiala, for instance, the houses of the Julahas and Sunars are even to date in proximity with the houses of the Jats and the Brahmans.

In urban areas the *mohallas* of the artisans and craftsmen generally remained separate.[10] In Amritsar city, for example, the area known as Bazaar Kaserian was resided mainly by the

---

link road connecting Jalandhar with Batala. Before 1947, there was a separate street occupied by the Kashmiris, known as Kashmirian- di-Gali. The other mohallas have continued to the present.

[7] In Amritsar district and in the neighbouring areas the term commonly used was the *thathi*, while in the districts of Hoshiarpur, Jalandhar and Ludhiana, the term *chamarhli* was used for the residential enclosures of the Chamars.

A Chamar working as a leather-dyer in a tannery told the researcher in an un self-conscious manner that they had their 'separate *chamarhli*'.

[8] Most of the residents claim to have been living there for a very long time, or as they say, 'from the beginning'.

[9] Kessinger, 52.

[10] Parkash Tandon also refers to separate *mohallas* of Lohars and Sunars: 15-85, 91.

Kaseras or utensil-makers.[11] In the narrow lanes which open out in the main bazaar a large number of workers from this particular caste can be seen even to date working on furnaces moulding raw metal into shining utensils of every size and use. The locality adjacent to this area was occupied by the Sunars and it was known as the Hira Market. Even to this date, the majority of the people working here are of the goldsmith caste. The Bazaar Sarafan[12] in Amritsar was occupied exclusively by the bullion merchants generally of the same caste. In the city of Gujranwala Bazaar Khandwala was inhabited exclusively by the Sunars. Similarly, even in small towns like Batala in Gurdaspur district there were separate *mohallas* of different artisans pursuing different occupations. The masons lived in Rajarian-di-Gali, the ironsmiths had their own locality with a separate mosque; the makers of brass utensils had their own *mohalla* called *thathiaran mohalla*; the potters had their separate *mohalla*; the weavers too lived in a distinct locality of their own. The tanners and leather dyers, however, lived away from the town or in an area where the movement of the people was not frequent.[13]

On the whole it seems that the Khatris, Brahmans and the Jats, preferred not to have any Lohar, Kumhar, Julaha or Mochi in their neighbourhood. But, to the Sunars and, to some extent, the Tarkhans, because of the nature of their work and better economic conditions, this reservation did not apply. Those Chamars who had adopted weaving as their profession were also permitted to reside within the village.[14] The separateness of the residential areas between the lower and upper castes also implied the absence of any informal relations between them in the conventional situation.

[11] Kasera is a caste of the makers of vessels of copper, brass and other mixed metals: Ibbetson, 317.

[12] Persently called Guru Bazaar.

[13] Even to date the *mohallas* of Thathiars, Lohars and Tarkhans exist in the town: See also Grewal (1975), 20.

[14] Author's interview with Dr. Gurdial Singh Phul. He was a prominent Punjabi play-write and stage director. He belonged to village Nangal-Shama in Jalandhar district.

In the altered conditions, which began to be noticed in the 1860s, the differences in occupations, income and general social standing began emerging among the artisan castes. Their improved economic standing had important consequences for social relations with the upper castes and within the kin-group and the parent caste.[15]

In their interviews the vertically mobile artisans revealed that those who had abandoned their traditional occupations chose not to maintain any link with the parent group. They did not even permit any of their close relatives or direct blood relations from the exogamous group (*got*) to continue in the traditional caste occupation. A retired inspector of industries, a Chamar by caste, stated that his grandfather worked neither as a leather-worker nor as a field labourer.[16] He could not recall if any one from amongst their relatives worked in leather. Rather, his family and relatives deliberately avoided having any link with those who preferred to continue to work in leather. They would'nt even permit any leather-worker to reside in their neighbourhood. The respondent also added that his father was the first weaver who worked for a merchant of Hoshiarpur and later on became a middleman between the same merchant and other weavers.

Another respondent belonging to the Chamar caste and working as a leather-dyer admitted that those of his kin who had abandoned leather dyeing or tanning would not maintain any link with those who still worked in leather. As a result all of his close relatives now were either tanners, leather-dyers or shoe-makers.[17] Similarly, out of all the Tarkhans interviewed,

[15] See Saberwal, 107.

[16] The respondent belongs to village Toto-Majra in Hoshiarpur district. Presently a manager in an industrial concern in Jalandhar city. His forefathers had taken to weaving because it was considered 'socially disgraceful' to work in leather. All of his relatives, he informed, were either in government service or in business. One of his uncles migrated to Canada during the 1920s.

[17] This leather-dyer belonged to village Garh Shankar in Jalandhar district. He has his entire kin group engaged in tanning, leather-dressing and leather-dyeing. He himself is engaged as a leather-dyer in a sports goods manufacturing and leather-tanning concern in Hoshiarpur.

more than 80 per cent confirmed that all of their relatives were carpenters. In another instance, a Ramgarhia who held an executive post in a cotton mill in Bombay did not acknowledge his poor relatives. One of the boys among his relations who stayed with him was asked to live in a store room. He was allowed entry in the house only from the back side.[18] Among the Ramgarhias of Modelpur in Jalandhar district, the wealthier ones would not even attend the marriages of the sons and daughters of the caste fellows with lower economic standing.[19] In short, those artisans who still retained their traditional occupations no longer had any social interaction with even the kinsmen who had moved out of the traditional occupation. In fact, with a section of the caste people becoming wealthier, the unity of the caste tended to decline.[20] With increasing differentiation in occupations among the members of each caste the reciprocity of cash payments and gifts at wedding ceremonies called *neonda* was also losing significance.[21] It was customary to offer cash as gift on occasions of marriages which was recorded in the account books of the family with the expectation of reciprocity. But since reciprocity was based on equality and mutual regard, the customary gifts on ceremonial occasions lost all meaning.[22]

There are, however, some instances to the contrary as well. Sometimes, the successful members of the artisan castes were obliged to retain their base with the parent kin group in the village under the compulsion of the circumstances. A college

[18] Saberwal, 107.

[19] Saberwal, 105.

A similar situation arose among the Bhils of southern Rajputana in the early 1920s when a section of the Bhils under the influence of a reform movement known as the Bhagat movement would not maintain any social relations with the non-Bhagat Bhils. The non-Bhagat Bhils ate meat and drank liquor and the Bhagats were vegetarians: Vashishtha (1992), (Mimeographed).

[20] Saberwal, 107.

[21] *neonda* means a gift or cash from relatives or friends on social ceremonies, particularly, marriage.

[22] Saberwal, 108.

teacher of Gurdaspur, Tarkhan by caste, whose grandfather had become an agriculturist admitted that had the circumstances been otherwise he too would have left the village and drifted away from the *biradri* like others.[23] He could not do so because he owned land and because he needed the support of his *biradri* to counter the repulsive and arrogant behaviour of the Jats towards his father and other low-caste land-owners whom they did not tolerate in their neighourhood on a footing of social equality.

Still another aspect of retaining ties with the basal kin group by the successful members was to pull the fellow caste people out of their traditional locality and enable them to benefit from the new opportunities. The group thus weaned away would gradually get transformed into a distinct endogamous group.[24] This process became evident from what an affluent Ramgarhia respondent of the city of Amritsar explained.[25] The father of the respondent being a qualified mechanical engineer was employed by the Tata Iron and Steel Mills at Jamshedpur in the early 1920s. Since the factory was fast expanding this engineer invited the whole of his kin-group who lived in a suburb of Amritsar to come to Tata Nagar to work at the factory initially as mechanics and fitters and later on, also as engineers. This group, gradually acquired a distinct character. In the earlier stages, they maintained some link with their caste fellows in the Punjab as they had to marry their sons and daughters. Gradually, after about a generation or a span of twenty years, this link too was broken when they did

[23] The respondent has a doctorate in literature and teaches in a college. He belongs to village Dadwan in Gurdaspur district. His grandfather had purchased about ten acres of land and had taken to agriculture. The grand father did his own repair work, but not for others.

[24] Risley also noticed the tendency of the formation of new endogamous groups among several Rajput castes. When the members of a caste left their original habitat and settled permanently in other parts of India, they developed into a distinct sub-caste: 88.

[25] The respondent's, in fact, is the only family living in the Punjab. He is a prominent industrialist of Amritsar. His father was stated to be the first qualified Indian engineer with the Tatas. His replies were helpful in understanding the social situation in rural areas located on the urban fringe.

not have to depend on their caste fellows in the Punjab even for matrimonial ties. As a self-contained endogamous group, they had members of nearly equal social and economic standing and the uniting element was their shared background and the present locale.

In such a situation involving spatial mobility on the part of a kin group, changes in social relations within the caste or with the parent group became more manifest. The dispersion of the members of a caste led to the disunity of the caste and kinship group, but endogamy remained the basic principle of matrimony for those who had moved away from the parent group, thus providing a sense of roots and cohesion to the mobile people. They tended to detach themselves from the parent body in stages and after moving away from their exogamous groups formed another endogamous group.

The process of dissociation from the parent group usually began by first moving away from the residential enclosure of the parent caste group and also ceasing to enter into new commitments for matrimonial relationships. This would reduce the frequency of visits to the earlier locality. After a few years of gap, the intimacy of relations was replaced by mere informality; and further by only formal relationships.[26] After a gap of another five to ten years, the mobile individual or group would be completely dissociated from the parent group. It would not be incorrect to say that the formal relationship between the mobile persons and the parent caste and kin group existed only upto the first generation. The second generation knew very little about the erstwhile kin group. The new endogamous group thus formed was composed of the caste fellows with similar socio-economic standing, and rigidly confined its matrimonial ties within the

[26] By 'informality of relationship' we mean observance of reciprocity of goodwill, exchange of views on common problems of the locality or the village, whereas intimacy of relationship was indicated by frequency of visits to one another's house, participation in social ceremonies and the exchange of *neonda* or gifts and cash on marriages. The 'formal' relationship implies exchange of visits only by invitation at marriages and deaths and very little interaction in normal routine.

group. This new group aspired to develop formal, informal and intimate relations with the members of the target group or those whose occupation they had joined.

III

The vertically mobile persons from amongst the artisan castes sought the acceptance of the target group in particular and the upper castes in general through a variety of ways. In order to achieve the status of a non-polluted caste the lower caste groups, the Chamars, for instance, would stop eating carrion or beef. The Chamars of Rampur, after having stopped eating carrion, secured their entry into the houses of the agriculturist families.[27] Similarly, in village Madhopur in Jaunpur (Bihar) the Chamars not only decided against eating beef, but also refused to carry animal waste to the fields. Their women refused to make dung cakes for agriculturists' households.[28] These changes did not make themselves felt in a short period of time. In Rampur it took more than a generation for the Jats to appreciate the change by allowing the Chamars to enter into their houses.[29] In Madhopur it took more than two generations for the upper castes to allow the Chamars a higher social status. As Cohn remarks 'while the *Camars* are becoming stricter about their habits of diet, dress and occupation, the higher castes are becoming less strict. *Camars* have become very sensitive about such matters as accepting food from castes whom they consider to be inferior, while at the same time some of the *Thakurs* are relaxing their conformity to commensal prohibitions'.[30]

At the same time, however, under the new circumstances, the mobile members of the artisan castes were incresingly becoming aware of their low social evaluation and the accompanying economic subordination. Many of them tried

[27]Rampur is located near Delhi and the study was conducted by an anthropologists. See Lewis, 40-41.

[28] Cohn, 72-75.

[29] Lewis, 41.

[30] Cohn, 73.

to protest against this by displaying the tokens of their better economic condition usually in the form of a *pacca*-house, good clothing and expensive wedding ceremonies. But their attempts at improving their status were thwarted by dominant castes, particularly the Jats in the countryside, who expressed their superiority in several ways.

Ibbetson's observation in 1881 that 'till quite lately, Jats and like would smoke with him (the Tarkhan) though latterly they have begun to discontinue the custom' indicates that upto about the last quarter of the nineteenth century the Jats and the 'clean' castes among the artisans had harmonious social relations but that fissures were beginning to develop in this.[31] The respondents, when questioned specifically about this, said that by the 1920s the Jats appeared to be particularly conscious of their superior social position vis-a-vis the artisans than ever before.

The land-owners repeatedly reminded the artisans of their low status and told them to remain within their limits. It was considered derogatory by a Jat land-owner to have any person of an artisan caste as a neighbouring land-owner. As mentioned by the Lohar resident of village Dadwan referred to earlier, the neighbouring Jat land owners used to harass his father on one pretext or the other. One of the methods used was to block the irrigation channel when it was the Lohar's turn to irrigate his fields. On several occasions he was obstructed from taking his turn to irrigate the fields. The Jats once implicated the respondent in a criminal case also. The respondent, however, was acquitted of the charges but the tension between them continued until recently. This was the major reason because of which the respondent could not severe his connections with his *biradri*. The petty local officials also harassed this respondent's father by obliging him to do *begar* for them. The respondent's father had stopped working as a carpenter and blacksmith, but the Patwari, Zaildar and other local officials continued to ask him to repair their doors, windows and cots (*Charpai*).

[31] Ibbetson, 313.

The Jats sometimes used their position as village officials to harass the affluent artisans. The practice of the collection of the tax called *khush-haisiyat* was prevalent in some parts of the Punjab. The tax was collected by local village officials and remitted to the funds of the District Board. It was levied only from prosperous non-agriculturists. It was 'entirely at the discretion of the local officials to recommend the names of prosperous residents to be brought on to the list of tax payers'.[32] The son of a respondent explained that whenever a Lohar or Tarkhan attained some affluence which offended the *Jats*, they retaliated by recommending to the officers of the District Board visiting the village that the 'offender' be taxed at a rate which he was not in a position to pay.[33] The idea behind the ill treatment of the artisans seeking to change their occupation and social status was to discourage the members of this *Kati-wadi-biradri* from aspiring for equality with the Jats.[34]

As pointed out above, during the 1920s and the 1930s the mechanized industry had been developing rapidly and so was the number of factories and the operatives. At this time, the Lohars, Tarkhans, Chamars and members of other artisan castes were benefitted also by the new constructions in towns and cities in India and abroad. Those who acquired some wealth sent it back to their families. The money thus accumulated was generally spent on good clothing, housing, and other symbols of better or upper caste living. The affluence of the low castes was seen as threat by the upper castes to their traditional dominance in social and economic spheres.

In the early stages of the new-found affluence, however, it

[32] A respondent of the Lohar caste of village Sathiala in Amritsar district informed about this tax. His great grandfather served under Maharaja Ranjit Singh as a manufacturer of arms and ammunition. The *karkhana* (manufactury) was in village Sathiala itself. The premises of the *karkhana* were later converted into a floor mill.

[33] The respondent was a victim of this situation.

[34] This signified traditional prejudice against those who worked with hands and tools. The Tarkhans and Lohars were called *kati-wadi-biradri* because they would often hurt themselves in the course of pursuing their occupations and even cut their fingers or toes: Saberwal, 99.

was difficult for any one of the artisan castes to construct a *pacca*- house, as generally only the Lambardar and rich land-owners owned *pacca*-houses in villages.[35] The construction of a house by a low caste would certainly contribute towards the development of tension between the Jats and the artisans. The Jats did not tolerate such a development, even if they earlier had amicable relations with their *kamins*. The case of village Nangal-Shama of district Jalandhar may illustrate further. The respondent of the Tarkhan caste explained that his family had extremely cordial relations with the Jats of the village and visits to one another's house were frequent and informal. The respondent's father was addressed as *chacha* or *taya* (younger or elder brother of ones father). They shared one another's grief and happiness.[36] But when he started the construction of a *pacca*-house in 1932, the Jats began to obstruct the work of construction on one pretext or the other. The respondent wanted to raise a second storey also, with a *chaubara* as part of the front elevation.[37] The Jats objected to this by saying that it would be used for gazing at the ladies of the adjoining houses. The matter was referred to the village Panchayat. It was only after the assurance to the villagers before the Panchayat, that the *chaubara* would not be 'misused' that the respondent was allowed to complete the construction. Incidentally, earlier, the Lambardar alone had a *pacca*-house in that village. Similar cases can be cited from villages near Modelpur, where a land-owner obstructed the construction of a house by a Ramgarhia on a plot he had bought.[38]

There, nevertheless, are some indications that the social relations between the upper castes and the members of the artisan castes who had changed their occupations after

[35] To own or to build a new *pacca*-house in a village was considered to be the prerogative of affluence and power which also signified superior social status.

[36] See n. 14 above. The respondent lived in Amritsar after his retirement as the principal of a college.

[37] *Chaubara* is an upper storey room with four doors and overhead projection on the front.

[38] See Saberwal, 99.

obtaining education were developing in a somewhat different direction. Most of the educated respondents of the districts of Gurdaspur, Jalandhar and Amritsar who were living in urban areas or the urban fringe were emphatic that in schools and colleges they were not discriminated against. A Chamar respondent of Jalandhar district informed that his classmates did not mind coming to his house; though they did so stealthily, apparently against the wishes of their elders.[39] The Tarkhan respondent of Dadwan village had close friendship with one of his class mates of the Jat caste which has continued to date and which he attributed to their similar tastes and interests in literature. An industrialist respondent of Amritsar belonging to Tarkhan caste could not recall if his teachers or fellow students ever passed any derogatory remarks on him.

IV

The quest for new occupations and an altered social status was aided also by the census operations. The censuses provided the members of the artisan castes with an opportunity to register their changed socio-economic position. Those artisans who had changed their occupations would return themselves as belonging to the caste whose occupation they had adopted. This was first noticed by Ibbetson in 1881 when some lower caste groups, who had taken to agriculture, returned themselves as Jats.[40] The census reports of 1891, 1901, 1911

[39] See n. 17 above. The respondent attended the school upto 5th standard.

[40] The following are the figures of those artisans who returned themselves as belonging to Jat caste in the districts to Multan, Jhang, Montgomery, Muzaffargarh, Dera Ismail Khan and Dera Ghazi Khan:

Original Caste	*Number of Claimants of Jat Caste*	*Original Caste*	*Number of the Claimants of Jat Caste*
Julaha	4,243	Kumhar	5,354
Tarkhan	6,730	Lohar	2,332
Zargar (Sunar)	21	Mochi	11,158

Source: Ibbetson, 106-107.

and 1921, however, do not provide data on this point.[41]

According to the census policy of 1901, castes were to be tabulated in an hierarchical order in accordance with their social evaluation.[42] In 1911, the census superintendent noted an attempt on the part of the educated sections of the Tarkhans, Lohars and some other artisan groups, to claim upper caste status, preferably that of the Rajputs and the Brahmans.[43] In 1931, however, a large number of the members of the artisan castes expressed their desire to be included among the Jat, Rajput, Pathan and Brahman castes. It was possible to detect such cases because the enumerators were instructed to put the original caste of the claimants in brackets so that they could be counted among the people of their original castes.[44]

Majority of the claimants for the 'upper' caste status actually returned themselves as belonging to one agriculturist caste or the other. This was in contrast with the tendency noticed in other parts of India where the Brahman and Kshtriya status was the most favoured one among the low-caste aspirants for a higher social status.[45] In the Punjab 44 per cent of the aspirants for the upper caste status from amongst mostly the Sunars, Mochis, Kumhars, Julahas and the Lohars, sought for themselves the status of the Rajputs. About 8 per cent of the aspirants, belonging mostly to the Mochi, Kumhar and the Julaha castes, sought the Jat status. The Lohars and the Tarkhans, in all probability from the Kangra hill region, were an exception in seeking the status of Brahmans.[46] It appears that those who had either already acquired land or were interested in purchasing land wished to be counted among the agriculturist castes in their respective

[41] Sharma (1979), 252-57.

[42] *Progs. Home (census) - A, June 4, 1901*, File No. 2-13.

[43] *Census Punjab 1911*, pt. I, 394.

[44] *Census Punjab 1931*, pt I, 325.

[45] In 1931 in United Provinces, Bengal, Sikkim, Bihar, Orissa, Central Provinces and Berar, out of 148 castes, Kshtriya status was preferred by 80 castes, and 33 castes preferred Brahman status: Srinivas (1977), 99.

[46] The number of persons of artisan castes who returned themselves as belonging to the upper castes:

localities to fulfil the qulifications laid down by the Punjab Alienation of Land Act 1900.

The shift from one social status to another by way of registering change by means of census operations or by any other means pointed to the changing socio-economic position of the lower castes under the Raj. It was as much a sign of the new aspirations as of growing consciousness of their disabilities. It was, probably, also a defensive device on the part of the economically better off artisans to ward off or withstand the repulsion of the upper castes. The repulsive attitude and behaviour of the upper castes obliged majority of the mobile artisans to come closer to one another and in certain cases come up with socio-political organizations like the Ad-Dharm Mandal.

Original Caste	*Total Aspirants*	*Preferred Upper Caste Status*					
		Awan	*Jat*	*Rajput*	*Sheikh*	*Khatri*	*Brahman*
Chamar	43,114	1,277	20	112	-	-	-
Julaha	16,511	1,277	3,706	8,511	1,776	-	11
Kumhar	5,279	594	1,236	2,856	100	31	1
Lohar	5,136	440	677	2,328	450	54	1,003
Mochi	9,411	421	2,634	5,516	484	2	-
Sunar	35,370	7	281	33,001	59	2,022	20
Tarkhan	14,199	691	1,377	4,447	360	2,022	7,021
Total	1,29,020	4,407	9,931	56,771	3,229	4,132	8,056

Source:*Census Punjab 1931*, Pt I, 364-65.

CHAPTER SEVEN

Social Change and Political Articulation

The changes in the structure of social and economic relationships between the artisan and other castes and among the artisan castes themselves were the cumulative result of the developments in economic, political, socio-religious, and educational spheres under colonial rule in the Punjab. In the new situation the services of village artisans became less remunerative and new opportunities of employment were also beginning to be available. The artisans, therefore, began to move towards new occupations in the village and out side. The spatial and occupational mobility signified change in social relationships which had political implications as well. Most of the changes became evident in early decades of the twentieth century. For appreciating this change, we need to quickly review the objective and subjective social, economic, and political realities in the Punjab under the British from the perspective of the lower castes in general and the artisans in particular.

I

The artisans constituted nearly one-fifth of the total population of the Punjab. Important among them, numerically as well as according to the nature of work performed, were the Lohars, Tarkhans, Julahas, Kumhars, Chamars and Mochis and the Sunars. The Chamars were the largest forming about 24 per cent of the total among them; they were followed by the Julahas, Tarkhans, Kumhars and Lohars. Because of the general nature of their occupations and their economic subservience to the land-owners, the artisans were called *kamins* or menials, and were universally considered socially low. Majority of them happened to be Muslims but whether Muslim, Hindu or Sikh, they were broadly treated at par with the *sudra* of the Hindu *varna* system. The Chamars and Mochis, however, were considered untouchables.

The majority of the artisans were concentrated in the countryside of the well cultivated and more populous districts of the central Punjab plains. The concentration of the artisans in the agriculturally well developed areas was obviously due to their usefulness in all sorts of agricultural operations from sowing to reaping and selling of the crop. The articles of wood and metal like the ploughs, yokes, sugar-cane presses, sickles, axes, spades, boiling pans and the handles to various implements were manufactured by the Tarkhans and the Lohars. The Chamars and Mochis provided the articles of leather like the leather-thongs as well as the blinders for the bullocks driving the persian wheel and the sugar-cane press. They also removed the hides and skins from the dead cattle and worked as tanners and leather-dyers. The household vessels and *tinds* (earthen pots tied round the persian wheel to draw water from wells for irrigation) were supplied by the Kumhars.

The artisans provided the services and furnished agricultural implements to the village society according to their specialized skills under the arrangement generally known as the *sep* or the *jajmani* system and shared with the land-owners mutual obligations for work and payment. They had fixed duties assigned by tradition. The most important among them like the carpenters, blacksmiths and the potters, whose assistance in agricultural operations was vital, were considered superior or the *vade kamins*, and the leather-workers or the Mochis and the Chamars were acknowledged as *laude* or the inferior *kamins*.

The remuneration of artisans was determined by local customs and they were paid in kind by a fixed share of the produce from land. The blacksmiths, carpenters and potters were paid at almost the same rates. At each harvest they received one sheaf of corn weighing about a maund and six seers of grain per house. They were also allowed to have the last pickings of cotton. In addition, the blacksmith received two *tinds* of sugar-cane juice daily when employed for making the boiling pan; he also received a ball of *gur* (unrefined sugar) while the sugar-cane press was in operation. The carpenter was paid one rupee and four annas for making the sugar-cane press (*velna*) and keeping it in order. The Chamars and Mochis were paid at half the rates of the Tarkhans, Lohars and Kumhars. The cumulative dues of the artisans under the *sep* system—generally 10 to 16 per cent—were deducted from the total produce of the village before making any other payment.

On social occasions, like marriages and births, the artisans made ritual accessories for their patrons for which they were entitled to a fixed fee known as the *lag,* and were called the *lagis*. Clothes and ornaments were furnished by the weavers and goldsmiths. They, however, did not come under the *sep* system and were paid according to specific services. The artisans, barring the goldsmiths perhaps, were employed during the sowing and reaping of the harvest as field labourers. They were paid separately for serving in their non-professional capacity for the weeding, reaping, threshing, sifting and stacking of the crop. The Chamars were expected also to work on *begar* or unpaid labour because of which they were called the *begaris*. The *begar* included carrying the fodder for cattle from the fields; white-washing the village guest-house; carrying the luggage of the visiting officials from one place to another, and attending to their comforts during their stay in the village.

The artisans barely subsisted on the meagre payments received for performing various professional and non-professional services. They were the first victims of any failure in crops caused by famines, floods, droughts or epidemics. Being the poorest and living a hand to mouth existence they did not have the means to tide over the difficult phases. The chances of an average artisan to supplement his income by working outside the village or by supplying goods to the neighbouring towns and villages too were not many. Within and outside the *sep* system, the artisans, thus, depended upon the agriculturists who had an upper hand in the traditional economic and social relationships in the village.

The artisans, particularly in large villages and in towns and cities, were expected to live within their separate residential enclosures which were known according to their castes, such as *loharan-di-gali* and the *tarkhana-di-gali.* The Chamars lived away from the main village site and their residential locality was called *chamarhli.* Even when the artisans understood their low economic level and corresponding social status was because of the nature of their work, they continued to work in the same capacities because the system guaranteed them a living, and also perhaps because the landowning castes would not easily allow them to move outside the *sep* system. Moreover, at the outset of British rule, there had been very few openings for the artisans outside the traditional relationship.

II

Considerable inroads into the traditional socio-economic set up were made within a few decades of British rule. With the extension of agriculture and its increasing commercialization—supported by the development of the means of communications—the villages were more effectively integrated with markets within and outside the Punjab. Under new conditions the agriculturists produced for sale in the market for cash. By the 1920s, market purposes dominated the nature of cultivation in all the well developed agricultural regions of the province. At the same time, greater interaction between the urban and rural areas facilitated the infiltration of factory-made goods and mill-made cloth into villages hitting directly the income of village artisans. For example, by the beginning of the 1860s increasing import of mill-made cloth from England was superceding the hand-loom fabrics produced by the village weavers. The carpenters and blacksmiths were now meant only to instal, repair and furnish the spare parts of persian wheel, not manufacture it. Increased recourse to canal irrigation and the influx of metal vessels for persian wheel and domestic use restricted the services of Kumhars as regular *sepidars*. The leather-workers were also caught in the vortex of change. The land-owners now preferred not to hand over the hides of the dead cattle to the Chamars and Mochis which was earlier their perquisite. The tendency was to sell the hides of dead cattle in the market for a cash price; these were tanned by tanneries to meet the demand within the country and abroad. The demand for articles made by local leather-workers also was steadily decreasing. The introduction of mechanical modes of transportation for long distance journeys caused reduction in the demand for harness and saddlery. The introduction of European type of footwear curtailed the demand for *desi* (indegenous) shoe. Purchase of good quality raw leather by big traders for export resulted in the import of tanned and dyed leather. The local leather-workers were left with only the inferior quality leather which made them incapable of competing in the market. In fact, by 1890 the Chamars were no longer regular *sepidars* in Amritsar, Lahore, Jalandhar and Gujranwala.

The unity and complimentarity between agricultural production and artisanal production in villages was thus disrupted and changes in social and professional relationships between the artisans and agriculturists became its natural corollary. The slackening of the age old economic relations, however, was slow. From regular exchange of services paid at each harvest it gradually moved towards the curtailment of the *haq-sep*, followed by its payment in cash and finally by the isolated exchange without any other obligation. With the decline in their regular income, the artisans were pushed out of their traditional socio-economic order to find new opportunities out side. The new opportunities — educational, economic and political — which were caste-free, atleast in theory, helped the enterprizing individuals and kin-groups among the artisan castes to pull out of their state of uncertainty and traditional bondage. Various developments like the colonization of land in canal colonies, extension of cultivation, development of the means of communications, commercialization of agriculture, growth of industry and the spread of literacy, provided them with new avenues of employment. By the turn of the twentieth century, percentage of the 'actually working' artisans who had abandoned their traditional occupations became rather significant: Chamars 67, Kumhars 48, Tarkhans 42, Lohars 45, Mochis 64, Julahas 36 and Sunars 16 per cent.

Since most of the artisans lived in rural areas, where agriculture was socially the most valued occupation, to turn to agriculture, preferably as land-owners or even as tenants, appeared to be the obvious avenue of change during the early years of British rule. By the turn of the century, a substantial number of them were recorded as engaged in agriculture. In 1911, 39 per cent of the 'actual workers' among the Chamars were enumerated as cultivators and field labourers. The Lohars and Tarkhans had, in fact, been continuing as agriculturists from the Sikh period; in their case the process was merely accelerated. The Punjab Alienation of Land Act 1900, however, hampered the acquisition of land by the thirfty village artisans. Now only those members of the artisan castes could purchase land who were not money-lenders and only if it was proved that the sale was not disadvantageous to the seller of the land.

The artisans eventually utilized this inability to tap other avenues of employment, particularly, by turning to industry as skilled and unskilled workers. Some Chamars, Lohars and Tarkhans were employed as skilled workers in cotton ginning and pressing factories; most of them worked as fitters and mechanics, and some even as engineers. The Chamars were employed in largest numbers as unskilled labourers in different industries. Many Chamars, Lohars and Tarkhans moved to distant parts of India in search of new opportunities. Outside the Punjab also, they largely continued their professions and were identified as the 'Punjabi mistris'. A good number of carpenters moved as far as to Assam to avail of new opportunities of work. They laid down the railway track or worked as contractors and labourers in plywood factories. The artisans of the Punjab were also able to exploit opportunities of employment in British colonies in Africa and

Latin America. They found their way to Brazil, Argentina, Cuba, the U.S.A., New Zealand, Fiji, Trinidad, Jamaica, Guiana, Malay Straits and Hong Kong.

Change of occupations by the artisans in the early stages was thus largely towards agriculture and later on towards industry where they could employ their skills and energies more effectively and advantageously. These changes, however, did not appreciably help them to improve their social evaluation. They continued to be evaluated with reference to their caste, which remained the source of frustration and discontent.

The increasing educational opportunities provided another avenue for change to the disoriented and discontented artisans. The possibility of employment in government offices and other establishments offering white-collar jobs encouraged the artisans to send their children to schools and colleges. The increasing literacy among the artisans may be understood as a sign of their desire for change, and the recognition on their part that education was the most effective means of achieving it. The educated among them went in for government service as civil, military and police personnel at lower rungs; some of them even became gazetted and commissioned officers in civil administration and also in the army and the police. A small proportion also took to professions as some became doctors, lawyers and teachers.

III

Occupational mobility among the artisan castes in the Punjab brought them face to face with new situations in their social relationships with other castes as well as within their own castes. The mobile artisans wanted to get out of the rut of social disabilities imposed on them for centuries. Those who had improved their socio-economic position tried to achieve a higher social status for themselves by borrowing customs, manners and eating habits of the groups traditionally superior to themselves. They spent money on good clothing and construction of *pacca*-houses. In the process they tended to move out of the localities they earlier lived in and to even dissociate themselves from the parent exogamous or kingroup. Their success, however, depended on the response of the higher evaluated caste groups. The attitudes of the upper castes particularly the landowning castes in villages, was generally repulsive. They discouraged the movement of the lower castes into their occupational sanctuary. The Jats, for instance, considered it a disgrace to have a *sepidar* of yester years in their neighbourhood cultivating land and aspiring for the same status as their own. They expressed their indignation over the upward mobility of their *kamins* on one pretext or the other. One of the frequently used methods was to block the canal water to the fields of the low caste neighbours and to implicate them in criminal cases. It was common to beat up a Chamar over trivial issues. They were implicated in false criminal cases. Even the construction of a *pacca*-house by a prosperous artisan was obstructed by the rich land-owners. To put it explicitly, those who changed their professions to become land-owners, teachers, lawyers, clerks and officers were unable to get recognition commensurate with their new occupations and improved economic conditions. This situation obliged the lower castes in general and the artisan castes in particular, to seek to transform the existing norms of social interaction through collective mobilization. The socio-political movements that emerged in the late nineteenth and early twentieth century among the lower castes, therefore, were based on the ideologies of challenge, protest and confrontation. The Ad-Dharm movement among the Chamars of the Punjab during the 1920s and the 1930s aiming at bringing about qualitative change in the structure of social relationships represented one such attempt.[1]

[1] Important backward class movements during this period were the 'Sri Narayan Dharma Paripalana' among the Izhavas, the agricultural labourers of Kerala, the Yadav movement organized as Gopal Mandali in 1901, and later on known as 'Gopjatiya Sabha' among the Ahirs and Yadavas of the then United Provinces and Bihar: Rao, (1979), 1-35. There was another low caste movement in South India known as the Adi-Dravid, among the Nadars of Tamilnadu: Hardgrave Jr., (1969). The other important backward class

IV

In the changed socio-economic conditions when social tensions were mounting, the socio-religious reform organizations held out hopes to the lower castes. The reform movements among Sikhs and Hindus endeavoured to recast the prevalent religious ideas and attitudes into forms suited to the requirements of the changing social order in the Punjab. The Arya Samajists, for instance, were opposed to ritual, superstition, irrational and anti-intellectual dogma in the traditional religions, they adopted the removal of untouchability, social taboos and caste hierarchy as important planks of their programme of social reform. They decried social inequalities and encouraged egalitarianism by inter-dining with the lower castes and by admitting them to schools.[2]

The Chamars were attracted first towards Arya Samaj. The educated and financially well off Chamars of Jalandhar and Hoshiarpur districts joined its subsidiary organization namely, Dayanand Dalit-Udhar Mandal at Hoshiarpur.[3] The prominent among them were Basant Rai, Thakar Chand, Mangu Ram and Swami Shudranand. Except for Shudranand they were all school teachers.[4] Gradually, however, they felt disillusioned as they suspected that the programme of social uplift of the untouchables was meant to keep them under the dominance of the caste Hindus.

They also understood that the social programmes of the reform organizations would ultimately strengthen the political leadership of the upper castes.[5] The Minto-Morley Reforms of 1909 and the Government of India Act 1919 envisaged

---

movements were among the Chamars of Bihar, Pallis of Tamilnadu, Mahars of Maharashtra and Kaivartas and Namsudras of Bengal: Sarkar 54-48.

[2] Jones, 202-03 and 303-11.

[3] Lala Devi Chand, a Khatri by caste was the president of Dayanand Dalit Udhar Mandal. The organization had pleaded in 1931 that the Ad- Dharmis should be counted among Hindus: *Home Department/Public, File, No. 45/67/31.*

[4] Juergensmeyer, 37-38.

[5] Bhatt, 66-98.

separate representation for Muslims and Sikhs in the Punjab.[6] Arya Samaj had sought to balance the numerical superiority of Muslims in the Punjab by enhancing the number of those who returned themselves as Hindu. Since the lower castes formed about one-fifth of the total population in the Punjab, they constituted a large reservoir of potential converts.[7] With the largest proportion of Chamars among the low caste non-Muslims, the Chamar leadership began to realize that they could become an important variable in the arithmatic of electoral politics.[8] They felt the need, therefore, to organize themselves separately from Hindus as well as Sikhs and to work for the socio-economic uplift of the Chamars.

Separation of the Chamars from Arya Samaj, it seems, was precipitated by a pamphlet published by the Ahmadiyas who did not appreciate the programme of social uplift by the Samaj.[9] They surmised that the programme was aimed at swelling its strength by using its lower caste members. They voiced this in a pamphlet entitled, *Acchut Udhar ki Haqiqat ya Hindu Aksari ke Mansube*, arguing that the uplift of untouchables was, in fact, a scheme for ensuring Hindu majority.[10] Swami Shudranand, who had earlier worked as the missionary of the Samaj now began to use the argument of the Ahmadiyas. In the wake of his tour of Jalandhar in 1925 a meeting was arranged with Basant Rai, Thakar Chand and others in which it was decided to form a separate organization under the name of Ad-Dharm Mandal. In 1926, Mangu Ram who was serving as a school teacher in village Mugowal in Hoshiarpur district was made its President and the Ad-Dharam movement was launched.[11]

[6] Khushwant Singh, Vol 2, 219-23.

[7] Jones, 288-89.

[8] Juergensmeyer, 22.

[9] Ibid., 74-82.

[10] Ibid., 40.

[11] Mangu Ram was earlier associated with the Ghadarites. He had gone over to the USA in 1909 through a labour contractor. He came into contract with the Ghadarites while he was in California and in 1915 he was entrusted by Sohan Singh Bhakna along with five other persons to carry a boat full of

The Ad-Dharm leaders evolved the ideology that the untouchables were a *qaum* distinct from Hindus, Sikhs and Muslims. They maintained that they were the original inhabitants of the land and that the Aryas came from outside and subdued them. Further, they tried to give a universal outlook to their ideology by claiming that as a religion Ad-Dharm did not belong to any particular caste, it was a religion of the people.[12]

The Ad-Dharmi leaders evolved a distinctive character for the '*qaum*'. They venerated Guru Ravi Das, a saint of the medieval period, who it is believed was a Chamar by caste.[13] They adopted a new salutation *Jai Guru Dev* (victory to the divine guru) to be replied by *Dhan Guru Dev* (Praise be to the divine guru).[14] By insistence on wearing red turban, they introduced an element of distinctive appearance.[15] Their organizational base was at Jalandhar with an executive body and secretarial staff. To propagate their ideology they published a journal, named the *Adi-Danka* (the pristine declaration). Like the Arya Samaj they also formed organized bodies of workers called *updeshaks* and *pracharaks* who travelled from place to place to spread the message.[16]

Having evolved the ideology of a distinct *qaum* and an organizational framework the Ad-Dharmis moved on to register their separation by means of census returns. In 1930, they represented before the government that Ad-Dharm should be listed as a separate religion in the forthcoming census of 1931. The request was conceded. Accordingly, nearly 2,50,000 Chamars out of the total of more than

arms to India. The boat was intercepted and Mangu Ram somehow managed to escape and was able to reach back to India in 1925. After his return he began to run an Arya Samaj aided school for the untouchables in his native village Mugowal: Juergensmeyer, 41-42.

[12] Juergensmeyer, 45-46.

[13] Bhakt Ravi Dass was a contemporary of Kabir and Guru Nanak: Darshan Singh, 33.

[14] Juergensmeyer, 53.

[15] We do not have satisfactory explanation as to why they preferred red colour.

[16] Juergensmeyer, 56.

7,70,000 returned themselves as Ad-Dharmis in the census of 1931. Nearly 70 per cent of the Ad-Dharmis belonged to the districts of Jalandhar and Hoshiarpur followed by Lyallpur, where they were nearly 9 per cent of the total.[17]

The Ad-Dharmis adopted an attitude of confrontation with the upper castes and attacked them in their conferences and rallies. They expressed their hostility towards the upper castes also by openly professing loyalty to the government in the hope of securing political and economic advantages for the Ad-Dharmis. Thus, the government was invoked alongwith God, and they pleaded that they should be given lands for cultivation.[18] The Ad-Dharmis also petitioned for government jobs and representation in the legislature, besides separate schools for their children or reserved seats for them in schools along with special scholarships.[19] Some of these demands were actually met by the government like free education to the depressed class children.[20] The Ad-Dharmi leaders sent delegations to the government commissions for public hearing, like the Simon Commission in 1929. Led by Mangu Ram they went to Lahore in large numbers to present their case. However, they could not meet the Commission. Later, Mangu Ram appeared as a witness before the Indian Franchise Commission in 1932. The Ad-Dharmis supported independent candidates in eight constituencies reserved for scheduled castes in the elections of 1936. The candidates supported by them won seven seats, albeit, with the support of the Unionists.[21]

[17] See chapter three above.

[18] Juergensmeyer, 134-35.

[19] This is clearly stated in the resolution passed by the All India Ad-Dharm Mandal, at Chak No. 241, Chanchal Singh Wala in Lyallpur district on March 19, 1931. The resolution contained the demands that action should be taken against those Hindus and Sikhs who had committed atrocities on them and that land be given to them so as their families could pull on well: *Home Department/Public, File No.* 205/31, dt. 20.3.1931.

[20] The government, in fact, had made education free for the children of the depressed classes and poor agriculturists in 1929: *Report on the Development of Education in the Punjab 1929-30.*

[21] Juergensmeyer, 138, 139.

The Ad-Dharmi leaders had mobilized support from their caste- brethern in their struggle for emancipation from the upper castes, and for social recognition, jobs and political favours. In the hope of help from the government they dissociated themselves from the national movement; rather, they 'offered full help on behalf of their organization for the safety of the Crown'.[22] By supporting the Ad-Dharmis the government succeded in alienating them from Arya Samaj and the Congress. In the process of their participation in the electoral politics the Ad-Dharmi leadership developed their own factional politics and as a corollary the issues and objectives for which the movement was launched were lost sight of. The movement continued with vigour till about the beginning of the 1940s after which it simply petered out and after the elections of 1946 its offices in Jalandhar were closed down in June. 'In abandoning religion for politics the Ad-Dharm leaders had abandoned the Ad-Dharm and the strength of its unifying symbol'.[23]

[22] *Home/Public, File No.205/31, dt. 20.3.1931.*

[23] Juergensmeyer, 152.

APPENDIX

Questionnaire

The questionnaire was prepared with a view to varify from the people of artisan castes their relations within their own caste groups and with the castes evaluated higher than theirs under the traditional as well as the changing situation during the colonial rule. The questionnaire is divided into two main parts: a proforma to elicit information about the antecedents of the respondents; and a questionnaire on educational and occupational history and on experiences within the *sep* system and after switching over to new occupations.

The respondents numbering about 100 were selected at random from urban and rural areas of the districts of Amritsar, Gurdaspur, Jalandhar and Hoshiarpur. Some of the respondents were migrants from several districts which are now in Pakistan. Most of the respondents were about 60 years; some of them were over 70 years of age. The respondents were drawn from all the major castes like the Chamar, Julaha, Kumhar, Lohar, Tarkhan, Mochi and the Sunar. The questionnaires were filled up after personally interviewing the respondents. They were given to understand that their names would be kept confidential.

Proforma

1. Respondent's Name:

2. Occupation: Present

   Previous/if any

3. Father's Name:

4. Occupation: Present

   Previous/if any

5. Address: Present

   Previous

6. The village, tahsil and district before the respondent migrated from rural area/or the respondent or his father migrated from Pakistan:

7. Biradri:

8. Education:

Questionnaire

I. OCCUPATIONAL HISTORY

A. 1. You are still continuing in your traditional occupation. Are you satisfied with the earnings from your work?

2. You shifted to your present occupation
   - (i) at what time?
   - (ii) under what circumstances?

3. After switching over to this occupation did you feel that you would be:
   - (i) able to make the best use of it in getting your children educated?
   - (ii) helping your children to get better jobs in government or any other institution?

B. 1. After the change in your occupation did your fellow caste men:
   - (i) feel jealous?
   - (ii) feel elevated?

2. What were your own feelings towards those: who felt jealous? felt elevated? who came to you for getting some work done in their favour in your office? requested you to absorb their men in some job?

3. After you became a shopkeeper/land-owner/tenant/factory owner/an employee of the government/ an employee of a private institution/a teacher/how did your colleagues in the occupation treat you:
   - (i) at par?
   - (ii) as an intruder in their territory?
   - (iii) as an outsider who should be ousted from the occupation?

4. Did the Patwari ever try to persuade you:
   (i) to make false statements?
   (ii) to pay money to get the right entries made in his record?

5. If you were a clerk in a government office, was the attitude of your officers:
   (i) humiliating?
   (ii) indifferent?
   (iii) hostile?

6. Is there any other information you would like to offer?

7. Can you refer to any one who had an experience similar to or different from that of yours?

II. EDUCATIONAL HISTORY

1. While in school or college what was the attitude of:
   (i) your teachers?
   (ii) your fellow students?

2. Did you ever feel that your caste was coming in the way of your pursuing your education?

3. At your going to school or college, did your relatives feel:
   (i) that it was useless?
   (ii) that it was no good?
   (iii) that their children should also do this?

4. The members of your caste who went to school :
   (i) did they do well in life?
   (ii) in what way?
   (iii) if not, why?

III. SOCIAL RELATIONS

A. 1. Was your position in your *biradri* due to:
   (i) your being an office bearer of a group or an association?
   (ii) your being close to a political leader?
   (iii) your official position in government, in bank, school, college or factory?

2. In the achievement of your success:
   (i) was the process smooth?
   (ii) were there any difficulties? how did you over come them?

B. Before 1947, how many persons of your *biradri* gained some important position or status? and how did they gain it?

C. Before 1947, did any person adopt a less dignified occupation than what was expected in your caste? under what circumstances?

D. 1. In the attitudes of the people, did you notice:
   - (i) any relaxation in terms of social communion?
   - (ii) any rigidity in terms of social communion?
   - (iii) did the upper caste people invite you to their place?
   - (iv) did they offer you tea, milk, *lassi* in the same mug or glass which they used for themselves?
   - (v) did they invite you on social occasions like marriage, or some other occasion in their families?
   - (vi) what was the reaction of Khatris/Jats/Brahmans/ Banias when you wanted to rent a house in their neighbourhood? Did you or any one in your *biradri* face any embarrassment or difficulty on this account?

2. Did you ever face any difficulty being a member of an artisan caste:
   - (a) at the courts and other government office?
   - (b) in getting a government job?

3. Do you attribute changes in attitudes of the people to political or social reform movements?
   - (i) what was the response of your caste fellows towards socio-religious movements like the Singh Sabha and the Arya Samaj?
   - (ii) have you come into contact with any leader of the movement?
   - (iii) were these movements responsible for the uplift of your caste?

IV. NET-WORK QUESITON / (Extension of social relations net work)

A. 1. Your interaction with the people of other social groups must have increased after change in your occupation and consequently in your position in society. Who were those encircled in the new net-work?
   - (i) their occupations?
   - (ii) their castes if you remember?
   - (iii) their position in their own caste group?

B. Do you retain relationships with the people of the traditional occupation of your caste?

V. KAMIN-ZAMINDARS RELATIONSHIPS

1. (a) did it continue as such during the British rule? yes or no?
   (b) at what time did you notice change?
   (c) were the Zamindars reluctant to pay *kamins'* dues?
   (d) was it due to additional employment opportunities available outside this relation-ship?

2. What was the mode and amount of payment to *kamins*? how much in grain and how much in cash? and how much for each service?
3. How did the land-owners feel at any *kamin's* progress?

VI. MIGRATION

A. 1. Did you think of migrating to town/city in your neighbourhood or some distant but big city? (i) under what circumstances?
2. Did any relative migrate to city? when and how many?
3. Did any of your relations migrate to any American, European or African country?
   (i) who and when?
   (ii) how did he manage to go (finances)?

4. What was the reaction of the upper caste men of your locality after he returned from abroad knowing that he was now well off?

Glossary

Arain:	An agricultural caste, living mainly in eastern Punjab and known for hard work.
Awan:	A land owning tribe in western Punjab.
Bair:	The wheel on which well pots (tinds) are strung.
Baniyan:	A mercantile caste.
Begar:	Literally means forced labour without payment; in actual practice undefined tasks for land-owners for nominal payment.
Bhari:	a sheaf (of unthreshed grain).
Chamar:	An untouchable caste of leather-tanners and workers.
Chamarhli:	Houses of the Chamars.
Chamrang:	A Leather-dyer.
Chaubara:	An upper room of a house, generally with four windows and an extended projection.
Charkha:	A spinning wheel.
Charpai:	A bed stead.
Chhimba:	A calico dyer.
Chuhra:	The lowest untouchable caste, generally scavengers.
Dabgar:	A maker of jars of hide.
Datri:	A sickle.
Ghara:	An earthen pitcher to store water.
Gur:	Un-refined sugar.
Hal:	A plough.
Jat:	The dominant agricultural caste in central Punjab.
Jajman:	Brahman's client or patron; the patron of a sepidar.
Jajmani:	The system of traditional relationship between the service performing manual workers and artisans, and the land owning cultivators involving mutual obligations of work and remuneration.
Kahi:	A spade.
Kalal:	A wine-distiller.
Kamin:	A village servant of low caste.
Karhaha:	A large boiling pan.
Karhni:	An earthen vessel to boil milk.
Khurpa:	An implement to cut grass by roots.

Kohari/Kohara: An axe.

Kudhi-Kamini: A cess on hearths realized by land-owners from non-agriculturist residents in villages. Also known as chulha tax or hearth tax.

Kumhar: The potter caste, spread all over the Punjab.

Lag: Reward for work done at various social and religious ceremonies by persons of artisan and menial caste.

Lagi: Persons of artisan and menial castes performing service on social occasions like marriage, betrothal, circumcision. They were paid for the services or the goods they provided on such occasions.

Lilari: A dyer.

Lohar: A blacksmith.

Mazhabi: The Sikh Chuhras who had abandoned their traditional occupation of scavenging.

Mirasi: A village bard, well known for his humour.

Mochi: A shoe-maker generally Muslim.

Nai: A barber; also called hajjam; he was generally the bearer of formal messages from one village to another.

Neonda: A gift or cash from relatives or friends on social ceremonies, particularly marriage.

Panjali: A yoke.

Patwari: Keeper of land records.

Penja: A cotton carder.

Pirhi: A low stool without a supporting back.

Raj: A mason.

Ramdasia: A Sikh Chamar.

Ramgarhia: A Sikh Tarkhan claiming links with the 18th century Sardar Jassa Singh Ramgarhia.

Sep: Hereditary relationship between agriculturists and village artisans and other menials under which the latter got a fixed share of crops.

Sepidar: A share holder under the sep system.

Siqligar: Metal burnishers, generally on the move and living in temporary huts.

Sunar: A goldsmith.

Tarkhan: A carpenter.

Touri: A small earthen pot used for cooking.

Teli: An oil-presser.

Thathera/ Thathiar: A metal worker, generally making vessels of copper and brass.

Thathi: Houses of the untouchables.

Velna: A wooden sugarcane crusher.

Zaildar: An officer of a group of villages.

Bibliography

PRIMARY SOURCES

1. Government Records

(i) ADMINISTRATION REPORTS

Selections from the Records of Government of India: II, *Report on the Administration of the Punjab for the years 1849-1850, 1850-51*, Calcutta 1853.

Selections from the Records of Government of India No.6: *General Report on the Administration of the Punjab Territories 1851-1852, 1852-1853,* Calcutta 1854.

Reports on the Administration of the Punjab and its Dependencies for the years: 1861-62, 1862-63, 1865-66 to 1869-70, 1871-72, to 1876-77, 1884-85, 1893-94, 1902-03, 1905-06, 1906-07, 1910-11, 1916-17 to 1933-34.

Reports on the Revenue Administration of the Punjab for the years between 1865-66 to 1934-35.

(ii) ASSESSMENT REPORTS

Canning, F.C., *Assessment Report Palwal Tashil, Gurgaon District,* November 1875.

Connolly, V., *Preliminary Assessment Report of Dehra and Hamirpur Tahsils of Kangra District,* Punjab Government Press, 1911.

Craik, H.D., *Assessment Report of Ajnala Tahsil of Amritsar District,* Punjab Government Press, Lahore 1913.

Fanshaw, H.C., *Assessment Report of Rohtak Tahsil, Rohtak District in the Revised Settlement 1873-1879*, MS.

———. *Assessment Report of Gohana Tashil, Rohtak District in the Revised Settlement of 1878*, MS.

Grant, J.A., *Assessment Report of Amritsar Tahsil in Amritsar District*

1892, Civil and Military Gazette Press, Lahore 1892.

Iftikhar-ud-Din, *Statements Relating to the Assessment of Hoshiarpur Tahsil of Hoshiarpur District,* Punjab Government Press, Lahore 1913.

O'Brien. E., *Assessment Report of Taluka Bhangal, Palampur Tahsil in the Kangra District 1890,* Civil and Military Gazette Press, Lahore 1891.

Purser, W.E., *Assessment Report of Jhajjar Tahsil in the Revised Settlement of Rohtak District 1878-79,* Lahore 1879.

———, *Volume of Returns Accompanying the Assessment Report of Tahsil Jhajjar in Rohtak District,* Part 2, nd MS.

———, *Volume of Returns Accompanying the Assessment Report of the Tahsil Sampla in Rohtak District*, MS.

(iii) CANAL COLONY REPORTS

Annual Reports of the Chenab, Jhelum, Chunian and Suhag Para Colonies for the year ending 30th September 1902, Civil and Military Gazette Press, Lahore 1903.

Annual Reports of the Chenab, Jhelum, Chunian and Suhag Para Colonies for the year ending 30th September 1903, Civil and Military Gazette Press, Lahore 1904.

Annual Reports of the Chenab, Jhang, Chunian and Jhelum Colonies for the year ending 30th September 1905, The Civil and Military Gazette Press, Lahore 1906.

Annual Reports of Punjab Colonies for the year ending 30th September 1923, Government Printing Press, Lahore 1924.

Annual Report of Punjab Colonies for the year ending 30th September 1924, Government Printing Press, Lahore 1925.

Punjab Colony Manual, Civil and Military Gazette Press, Lahore 1926.

(iv) CENSUS REPORTS

Hutton, J.H., *Census of India* 1931, Vol I: *India*, pt I, *Report*, Manager of Publications, Delhi 1931.

Ibbetson, Denzil Charles Jelf, *Report on the Census of the Punjab* 1881, Vol I, Calcutta; Vol II, Lahore 1883.

Kaul, Pandit Harkrishan, *Census of India 1911*, Vol XIV: *Punjab*, pt I & II, Civil and Military Gazette Press, Lahore 1912.

Khan Ahmad Hasan Khan, *Census of India 1931*, Vol XVII: *Punjab*, pt I & II, Civil & Military Gazettee Press, Lahore 1933.

Maclagan, E.D., *Census of India 1891*, Vol XIX: *The Punjab and its Feudatories,* pt I & II, Superintendent Printing India, Calcutta

1892.

Middleton, L.W. and Jacob, S.M., *Census of India 1921,* Vol XV: *Punjab and Delhi*, pt I & II, Civil and Military Gazette Press, Lahore 1923.

Punjab Government, *Selections from the Records of the Government of India No. XVIII: General Report on the Administration of the Punjab Territories from 1854-55 to 1855-56 Inclusive of Census Report of Punjab 1855,* J.F.Williams—Punjabee Press, Calcutta 1858.

———. *Report on the Census of Punjab taken on the 10th January 1868.* Indian Public Opinion Press, Calcutta, 1870.

Rose, H.A., *Census of India 1901*, Vol XVII: *The Punjab and its Feudatories and the North Western Frontier Province*, pt I & II, Government Printing Office, Simla and Lahore 1902.

Sheikh Fazl-i-Ilahi, Khan Bahadur, *Census of India 1941*, Vol VI, *Punjab*, Manager of Publications, Government of India, Delhi 1941.

Vashishtha, Lakshmi Chandra, *Census of India 1951*, Vol VII: *Punjab, Pepsu, Himachal Pradesh, Bilaspur and Delhi*, pt I-A, *Report*, Army Press, Simla 1953.

(v) DISTRICT GAZETTEERS

Ambala (1883-84); Amritsar (1883-84); Cheneab Colony (1904); Ferozepur (1888-89); Ferozepur, Statistical Tables (1935); Gujrat (1883-84); Gujrat (1892-93); Gujranwala (1883-84); Gurdaspur, Statistical Tables (1912); Gurgaon (1883-84); Hoshiarpur (1883-84); Jalandhar (1904); Jhang (1883-84); Jhang (1904); Jhelum (1883); Ludhiana (1888-89); Montgomery (1883-84); Mooltan (1883-84); Shahpur (1883-84); Sialkot (1883-84).

Imperial Gazetteer of India, Vol II: *Economic*, Clarendon, Press, London 1908.

(vi) MONOGRAPHS AND REPORTS OF THE DEPARTMENT OF INDUSTRIES

Monograph on Cotton Manufactures in the Punjab 1884, np nd.

Monograph on Wollen Manufactures of the Punjab 1884-85, Government Press, Lahore 1886.

Monograph on the Manufactures of Brass and Copper in the Punjab 1884-85, np nd.

Monograph on Wood Manufactures in the Punjab 1887-88, Civil and

Military Gazette Press, Lahore 1889.

Monograph on the Gold and Silver Works in the Punjab 1888-89, Civil and Military Gazette Press, Lahore 1890.

Monograph on the Pottery and Glass Industries of the Punjab 1890-91, Civil and Military Gazette Press, Lahore 1892.

Monograph on Leather Industry of the Punjab 1891-92, Civil and Military Gazette Press, Lahore 1893.

Monograph on Iron and Steel Industries in the Punjab 1906-07, Civil and Military Gazette Press, Lahore 1908.

Report on the Department of Industries Punjab for the year ending 31st March 1922, Government Printing Press, Lahore 1922.

Report on the Department of Industries Punjab for the year ending 31st March 1923, Government Printing Press, Lahore 1923.

Report on the Department of Industries Punjab for the year ending 31st March 1925, Government Printing Press, Lahore 1925.

Report on the Department of Industries Punjab for the year ending 31st March 1927, Government Printing Press, Lahore 1928.

Anand, Ram Lal, *Tanning Industry in the Punjab*, The Board of Economic Inquiry Punjab 1939.

Dhaliwal, Gurcharan Singh, *Agricultural Implements Industry of the Punjab*, The Board of Economic Inquiry Punjab, 1953.

Mahmood, M.H., *Report on the Industrial Survey of the Ludhiana District,* Government Printing Press Punjab, Lahore 1942.

Sodhbans, P.S., *Some Poorer Artisan Classes of Lahore 1941,* The Board of Economic Inquiry Punjab, 1941.

(vii) PROCEEDINGS OF THE GOVERNMENT OF INDIA

(A) *Foreign/Political:*

31 December 1847, 1832
September 1850, 77-81
February 1851, 37-44
March 1852, 533-35
December 1853, 204-06, 302
December 1854, 296-97
September 1855, 115-16
December 1855, 248-50
March 1858 (Secret)
December 1859, 78
General A, June 1862, 16-20
Revenue A, March 1864, 9-10
Revenue A, June 1864, 22.

(B) *Department of Commerce and Industry (Emigration):*

File No. 99 of 1905, 5-6
File No.73 of 1906, 13-16
July 1908, 10-12
September 1908, 22-23
December 1908, 23-25
May 1909, 1-3
March 1910, 1-2
September 1910, 6-10
November 1911, 1-3
April 1912, 42
May 1912, 1-6
August 1912, 14-15
April 1913, 19-24
File No. 168 of 1914, 7-15
April 1915, 5-6
November 1915 (Confidential)
April 1917, 26-41.

(C) *Department of Commerce and Industry (Industries):*

May 1905, 39-41
July 1905, 24
February 1906, 1
July 1908, 4
November 1910, 1-13
April 1916, 87
June 1916, 1-23
May 1917, 1

(D) *Department of Commerce and Industry (Factories):*

February 1906, file No.2 of 1906
October 1907, 3-16
December 1908, 1-18
November 1910, 1-13
November 1912, 1-16
May 1917, 1-7

(E) *Department of Industry and Labour (Labour):*

September 1922, 1-19 (i); July 1923, L-812 (6); L-924 (6), (7), (8), (9) of 1924, L-1174 (1) of 1924; L 2851 (14) of 1925; L-1174 (6) of 1926; L-1370 (1) of 1926; L-1174 (7), (8) of 1927; L-1174 (10) of 1928; L-1516 (1) of 1928; L-1174 (12) of 1929; L-1573 (3) of 1930; L-1759 of 1933.

(F) *Department of Industry and Labour (Industries):*

I-354 (2) of 1934; I-354(6) of 1935; I-354(9) of 1935; I-354(19) of 1936; I-354(41) of 1937; I-354(45) of 1937.

(G) *Home Department (Census): June 1901, 2-13.*

(H) *Department of Revenue and Agriculture (Agriculture):*

December 1882, 2-12
March 1883, 14-32
October 1883, 14-32
October 1884, 4-21
December 1888, 92-101
January 1890, 2-27
September 1891, 15-31
April 1892, 5-20
January 1893, 5-26
March 1894, 5-20
February 1896, 2-18
April 1897, 1-16.

(viii) REPORTS OF THE FAMINE COMMISSION

Punjab Report in Reply to Inquiries Issued by the Famine Commission 1878-79, vol. I, London, nd.

Report of the Indian Famine Commission 1878-79, Volume IV, London nd.

Report of the Indian Famine Commission 1898, Vol. III, Government Printing Office, Simla 1898.

Report of Indian Famine Commission 1901, Superintendent Government of India Printing Press, Calcutta 1901.

(ix) SETTLEMENT REPORTS

Bolster, R.C., *Final Report of the Fourth Regular Settlement of Lahore District 1912-1916*, Government Printing Press, Lahore, 1916.

Davies, R.H., *Report on the Revised Settlement of the Greater Part of the Goordaspur District 1856-1859 formerly known as Buttalla.* The Punjabee Press, Lahore 1859.

Davies, R.H. and Blyth, W., *Report on the Revised Settlement of Umritsar, Sowrian and Turn Taran Pargunnahs of Umritsar District in Umritsar Division,* Lahore 1860.

Douie, J.M., *Punjab Settlement Manual*, Civil and Military Gazette Press, Lahore 1899.

Dunlop-Smith, J.R., *Final Report of the Revision of the Settlement of Siálkot District in the Punjab 1888-1895,* Civil and Military Gazette Press, Lahore 1895.

Fagan, P.J., *Final Report of the Revision of Settlement of Montgomery District 1892-99,* Civil and Military Gazette Press, Lahore 1899.

Francis, E.B., *Final Report on the Revision of Settlement of Ferozepur District, Northern Parts 1884-1889*, Civil and Military Gazette Press, Lahore 1891.

Frayer, F.W.R., *Final Report on the First Regular Settlement of Dera Ghazi Khan District in the Derajat Division 1869 to 1874, A.D*., Central Jail Press, Lahore 1876.

Grant, J.A., *Final Report of the Revised Settlement of Amritsar District 1888-1893*, Civil and Military Gazette Press, Lahore 1893.

Ibbetson, Denzil Charles Jelf, *Report on the Revision of Settlement of Panipat Tahsil and Karnal Parganah of Karnal District 1872-80,* The Pioneer Press, Allahabad 1883.

Melwill, P.S., *Revised Settlement Report of Northern Parganahas and Some Portions of Ambala District*, The Chronicle Press, Lahore 1859.

Munshi, Amin Chand, *Report on the Revised Land Revenue Settlement of Hissar District in the Hissar Division of the Punjab,* Victoria Press, Lahore 1875.

———, *Report on the Revision of Land Revenue Settlement of Gujranwala District 1866-1867*, W.E. Ball & Co., Lahore 1874.

Purser, W.E., *Final Report of the Revised Settlement of Jalandhar District in the Punjab 1880-86*, Civil and Military Gazette Press, Lahore 1892.

Roe, C.A. & Purser, W.E., *Report on the Revised Land Revenue Settlement of Montgomery District of the Mooltan Division of the Punjab*, Central Jail Press, Lahore 1878.

Saunders, Leslie, S., *Report on the Revision of Settlement of Lahore District 1865-1869*, Central Jail Press, Lahore, 1873.

Walker, G.C., *Final Report on the Revision of Settlement of Lahore District 1893*, Civil and Military Gazette Press, Lahore 1894.

Walker, Gordon, T., *Final Report on the Revision of Settlement of Ludhiana District in the Punjab 1878-83*, Calcutta Central Press Co., Calcutta 1884.

Waterfield, *Report on the Second Regular Settlement of Gujrat District in the Punjab*, Central Jail Press, Lahore 1874.

Wilson, J., *Final Report on the Revision of Settlement of Shahpur District in the Punjab 1887-94*, Civil and Military Gazette Press, Lahore 1894.

Wynyard, W., *Revised Settlement Report on the Southern Paraganahs of Ambala District,* The Chronicle Press, Lahore 1859.

(x) VILLAGE SURVEYS

Ahmed, M. Bashir & Anand, R.L., *An Economic Survey of Jamalpur Sheikhan: A Village in Hissar District of the Punjab*, The Board of Economic Inquiry Punjab, 1937.

Anchal Dass, *An Economic Survey of Gajju Chak: A Village in Gujranwala District of the Punjab.* The Board of Economic Inquiry Punjab, 1934.

———, *An Economic Survey of Tehong: A Village in Jalandhar District of the Punjab*, The Board of Economic Inquiry Punjab.

Bhalla, R.C., *An Economic Survey of Bairampur: A village in Hoshiarpur District,* The Board of Economic Inquiry Punjab.

Brayne, F.L., *An Economic Survey of Bhandas: A Village in Gurgaon District of the Punjab*, The Board of Economic Inquiry Punjab, 1936.

Dawar, Lajpat Rai, *An Economic Survey of Suner: A Village in Ferozepur District of Punjab*, The Board of Economic Inquiry Punjab, 1936.

Gian Singh, *An Economic Survey of Gaggar Bhana: A Village in Amritsar District of the Punjab* (Survey No.1), The Board of Economic Inquiry Punjab, 1928.

Khan, Abdur Rahim, *An Economic Survey of Bhambu Sandilla: A Village in Muzaffargarh District of Punjab*, The Board of Economic Inquiry Punjab, 1935.

Randhir Singh, *An Economic Survey of Kala Gaddi Thamman: A Village in Lyallpur District of Punjab*, The Board of Economic Inquiry Punjab, 1932.

Seth, R.K. & Faiz Ilahi, *An Economic Survey of Durrana Langana: A Village in Multan District of the Punjab*, The Board of Economic Inquiry Punjab, 1938.

Sher Singh, *An Economic Survey of Naggal: A Village in Ambala District of the Punjab*, The Board of Economic Inquiry Punjab, 1932.

(xi) MISCELLANEOUS REPORTS

Provincial Report on the Moral and Material Conditions of the People of the Punjab 1881-91, Lahore 1892.

Memorandum on the Moral and Material Progress of India for the years: 1907-08 to 1911-12; 1913-14; 1920-21; 1933-34 to 1934-35.

Report of the Fact Finding Committee (Hand Loom and Mills), Government of India Press, Calcutta 1942.

Report on Internal Trade and Manufactures of the Punjab for the years 1880-81, 1881-82, 1882-83, and 1883-84, np nd.

Report of the Internal Trade of the Punjab for the years 1885-87, Lahore 1887.

Report on the Internal Trade of the Punjab by Rail and Rivers for the year 1921-22, Lahore 1923.

Report of Provincial Banking Enquiry Committee 1929-30, Vol I, Calcutta 1930.

Prices and Wages in India, 1900, Government Printing Press, Calcutta, 17th Issue.

Mukhtar Ahmed, *Report on Rickshaw Pullers of the Punjab*, Government of India Press, Simla 1946.

Cust, R.N., *Statistical Report of Amritsar Division*, Koh-i-noor Press, Lahore 1861.

Tuper, C.L., *Punjab Customary Law, Questions on Tribal and Local Customs: A Manual for the use of Settlement Officers*, Vol III, Calcutta 1881.

Reports on the Progress of Education in the Punjab for the years 1924-25 to 1947-48.

2. NON-GOVERNMENT CONTEMPORARY WORKS

Anand, Nihal Chand, *The Punjab Alienation of Land Act No. XIII 1900*, Amrit Book Company, Lahore 1924.

Anstey, Vera, *The Economic Development of India*, Longmans Green and Co., London 1949.

Ata-Ullah, *The Co-operative Movement in the Punjab*, George Allen and Unwin, London 1937.

Badenoch, A.C., *Punjab Industries 1911-17*, Government Printing

Press, Lahore 1917.

Bhattacharya, J.N., *Hindu Castes and Sects,* Editions Indian, Calcutta 1937 (first published 1896).

Briggs, Geo, W., *The Chamars*, B.R. Publishing Corporation, Delhi 1975 (first published 1920).

Baden-Powell, B.H., *The Origin and Growth of the Village Community in India*, New York 1908.

———, *Hand Book of the Manufactures and Arts of the Punjab,* Punjab Printing Co., Lahore 1872.

Darling, Malcolm Lyall, *The Punjab Peasant in Prosperity and Debt,* Manohar, Delhi 1977 (first published 1925).

Douie, James, *The Punjab, North-Western Frontier Province and Kashmir,* Cambridge University Press, Cambridge 1916.

Ibbetson, Denzil, *Punjab Castes*, Languages Department Punjab, Patiala 1970 (first published 1916).

James, E.D., *Primitive Ritual and Belief,* np 1917.

Risley, Herbert, *The People of India* (ed W. Crook), Oriental Books Reprint, Delhi 1969 (first published 1915).

Sherring, M.A., *Hindu Tribes and Castes,* Thacker Spink and Co., Calcutta 1879.

Trevaskis, Hugh Kennedy, *The Punjab of To-day: An Economic Survey of the Punjab in Recent Years (1870-1925)*, Vol. 2, Civil and Military Gazette Press, Lahore 1932.

Wilson, Sir James, *Recent Economic Development in the Punjab*, Richard Clay and Sons, Suffolk 1910.

Wiser, William H., *The Hindu Jajmani System,* Lucknow Publishing House, Lucknow 1958 (first published 1936).

SECONDARY WORKS

———, (Anon), 'The Punjab Weaving School', *Indian Review,* Vol XII, 1911, 652.

Adams, John, 'Studies of Indian Village Economy: A Bibliographical Essay', *The Indian Economic and Social History Review,* Vol VII, March 1970, 109-139.

Ahmad, Imtiaz, 'Caste Mobility Movements in North India', *The Indian Economic and Social History Review,* Vol VIII-2, June 1971, 164-191.

Ali, Imran, *Imperial Rule in the Punjab: 1885-1947*, OUP, Delhi 1989.

Arensberg, Conard, 'The Community Study Method', American *Journal of Sociology,* LX, 1954, 109-124.

Atal, Yogesh, 'The Case Study Approach in the Analysis of Short Range Social Change' (eds K.S. Mathur and Others), *Studies in Social Change*, Ethnographic and Folk Culture Society U.P., Lucknow 1973, 44-52.

Baij Nath, 'Some Leading Industries of Upper India', *Proceedings of Indian Industrial Conference,* Banaras 1905, 129-37.

Baij Nath (Lala), 'Some Factors in Industrial and Commercial Development of India', *Proceedings of Indian Industrial Conference,* Banaras 1905, 107-18.

Bailey, F.G., Caste and Economic Frontier - *A Village in High Land Orissa,* OUP, Bombay 1958.

———, *Tribe, Caste and Nation*, Manchester 1960.

Bal Krishan, 'Progressional Ruralization of the Punjab', *Report of the Ninth Indian Industrial Conference*, Amraoti 1913, 295-312.

Banerjee, Himadri, *Agrarian Society of the Punjab (1849-1901),* Manohar Publications, New Delhi 1982.

———, 'The Kamins of the Punjab', *The Panjab Past and Present,* Vol XI-II, 1977, 287-311.

Banga, Indu, *Agrarian System of the Sikhs*, Manohar Publications, New Delhi 1978.

———, 'Social Mobility in the Punjab Under Maharaja Ranjit Singh' (eds J.S. Grewal and Indu Banga), *Maharaja Ranjit Singh and His Times,* GNDU, Amritsar 1980, 125-37.

———, 'Polity, Economy and Urbanization in the Upper Bari Doab' (eds J.S. Grewal and Indu Banga), *Studies in Urban History*, GNDU, Amritsar 1981, 192-205.

, 'Karachi and its Hinterland Under Colonial Rule' (ed), *Ports and Their Hinterland in India 1700-1950,* Manohar, Delhi 1992, 337-58.

Banton, Michael, *Roles: An Introduction to the Study of Social Relations,* Tavistock Publication, London 1965.

Banvir Singh, 'Land Reforms and Social Change' (eds K.S. Mathur and Others), *Studies in Social Change,* Ethnographic and Folk Culture Society U.P., Lucknow 1973, 175-181.

Barber, Bernard, *Social Stratification: A Comparative Analysis of Structure and Process,* Harcourt Brace and World Inc., New York 1957.

———, 'Social Mobility in Hindu India' (ed James Silverberg), *Social Mobility in the Caste System of India*, Mounton, The Hague, 1968.

Barrier, N.G., *Sikhs and Their Literature*, Manohar Book Service,

Delhi 1970.

———, *The Punjab Alienation of Land Bill 1900*, Duke Univer-sity Press, Durham 1966.

———, (ed), *The Census in British India: New Perspective,* Manohar Publications, New Delhi 1981.

Beidlmann, Thomas O., *A Comparative Analysis of Jajmani System*, New York 1959.

Bendix, Reinhard and Seymour, Martin Lipset (eds), *Class, Status and Power: Social Stratification in Comparative Perspective,* Routledge and Kegan Paul, London 1947.

Beteille, Andre, *Caste, Class and Power,* University of California Press, Berkeley 1965.

Bhagat Singh, 'The Kuka Movement', *The Panjab Past and Present,* Vol VIII-I, 1973, 148-155.

Bhatia, B.M., *Famines in India (1860-1965)*, Asia Publishing House, Bombay 1967.

———, *History and Social Development,* Vol I: Elites in Modern India, Vikas Publishing House, Delhi 1974.

Bhatt, G.S., 'Occupational Structure Among the Chamars of Dehradun', *Sociological Annual*, Vol I, 1958, 32-43.

———, 'Ideological and Socio-Historical Role of Elites in the Brahmo Samaj and Arya Samaj Movements' (eds K.S. Mathur and Others), *Studies in Social Change,* Ethnographic and Folk Culture Society U.P., Lucknow 1973, 69-98.

Bipan Chandra, *The Rise and Growth of Economic Nationalism in India,* Peoples Publishing House, New Delhi 1969.

———, 'Presidential Address', *Proceedings Punjab History Conference 1981*, 6-18.

Chatterton, Alfred, 'Hand Weaving in India', *Indian Review*, Vol III, January-December 1902, 104-06.

Chaudhri, M.K.(ed), *Trends of Socio-Economic Change in India: Proceedings of a Seminar,* Indian Institute of Advanced Study, Simla 1969.

Chhabra, G.S., *Social and Economic History of the Punjab (1849-1901)*, Sterling Publishers, New Delhi 1962.

Chhibbar, Y.P., *From Caste to Class, A Study of Middle Classes,* Associated Publishing House, New Delhi 1968.

Chicherov, A., 'On the Multiplicity of Socio-Economic Structure in India in the 17th to the Early 19th Century', *New Indian Studies by Soviet Scholars, Social Sciences Today*, No. 33, 1976, 48-57.

Cohn, Bernard S. 'The Changing Status of a Depressed Class' (ed Mackim Marriot), *Village India*, University of Chicago Press, Chicago 1972, 53-77.

———, 'Chamar Family in a North Indian Village', *The Economic Weekly,* 13: 1961, 1051-1055.

———, 'Changing Traditions of a Low Caste' (ed Milton Singer), *Traditional India: Structure and Change*, Rawat Publications, Jaipur 1975, 207-215.

Coombes, 'The Hand Weaving Industry of India', *Indian Review*, Vol V, 1904.

Cox, Oliver Cromwell, *Caste, Class and Race: A Study in Social Dynamics,* Doubleday, New York 1948.

Damle, Y.B., 'Reference Group Theory with regard to Mobility in Caste' (ed James Silverberg), *Social Mobility in the Caste System in India*, Mounton, The Hague 1968, 103-14.

Drashan Singh, *A Study of Bhakta Ravi Dass,* Punjabi University, Patiala 1981.

Davis, Kingsley, *The Population of India and Pakistan,* Princeton, New Jersey 1951.

Den-David, Joseph, 'The Growth of Professional and Class System' (eds R. Bendix and Martin Lipset), *Class, Status and Power: Social Stratifiation in Comparative Perspective*, Routledge and Kegan Paul, London 1974, 459-72.

Desai, A.R., *Social Background of Indian Nationalism*, Popular Prakashan, Bombay 1966.

Dharma Kumar, 'Economic History of Modern India'. *The Indian Economic and Social History Review,* Vol IX, 1972, 63-90.

———, *Land and Caste in South India,* Cambridge University Press, London 1968.

———, (ed), *Cambridge Economic History of India,* Vol II: *1750-1947,* Cambridge University Press, Cambridge 1983.

Divekar, V.D. (ed), *Social Reform Movements in India: A Historical Perspective,* Popular Prakashan, Bombay 1991.

Domin, Dolores, *India in 1857-59: A Study in the Role of the Sikhs in the People's Uprising*, Akademie-Verlag, Berlin 1977.

Dungen, P.H.M. van den, *The Punjab Tradition: Influence and Authority in 19th Century India*, George Allan and Unwin, London 1972.

———, 'Changes in Status and Occupations in Nineteenth Century Punjab' (ed D.A. Low), *Soundings in Modern South Asian History,* Weidenfeld and Nicolson, London 1968, 57-94.

Dutt, R.C., 'Presidential Address', *Proceedings of First Indian Industrial Conference*, Banaras 1905, 1-5.

Eglar, Zekiye, *A Punjabi Village in Pakistan*, Columbia University Press, New York 1960.

Firth, Raymond, *Elements of Social Organization*, London 1957.

Floud, R.C., *An Introduction to Quantitative Methods for Historians*, London 1973.

Fauja Singh, *A Brief Account of the Freedom Movement in the Punjab*, Punjabi University, Patiala 1972.

———, *The Kukas*, Motilal Banarsidas, Delhi 1965.

Foddy, William, *Constructing Questions for Interviews and Questionnaire: Theory and Practice in Social Research*, Cambridge University Press, Cambridge 1993.

Ganguli, B.N. (ed), *Readings in Indian Economic History: Proceedings of the First All India Seminar on Indian Economic History 1961*, Asia Publishing House, Bombay 1964.

Ghurye, G.S., *Caste and Class in India*, Popular Book Depot, Bombay 1950.

Gould, Julius, Kolb, William, L., *A Dictionary of the Social Sciences*, Tavistock Publications, London 1964.

Grewal, J.S., *The Reign of Maharaja Ranjit Singh: Structure of Power, Economy and Society*, Punjabi University, Patiala 1981.

———, *The Sikhs of the Punjab*, Cambridge University Press, Cambridge 1990.

Grewal, J.S., Banga, Indu (Tr and ed), *Early Nineteenth Century Punjab: From Ganesh Das's Char Bagh-i-Punjab*, Guru Nanak (Dev) University, Amritsar 1975.

Grewal, Reeta, *Polity, Economy and Urbanization: Early, Nineteenth Century Punjab*, M. Phil. Dissertation, GNDU, Amritsar 1983.

Gupta, T.R., 'Rural Family Status and Migration', *The Economic Weekly*, Vol 13, 1961, 1597-1603.

Gurdarshan Singh, 'Origin and the Development of the Singh Sabha Movement', *The Panjab Past and Present*, Vol VII-I, 1973, 45-58.

Hardgrave Jr., Robert L., *The Nadars of Tamilnadu: The Political Culture of a Community in Change*, University of California Press, Berkeley 1969.

Haqood M.J., Price, D.O., *Statistics for Sociologists*, Henry Holt & Co., New York 1957.

Harbans Singh, 'Origins of the Singh Sabha', *The Panjab Past and Present*, Vol VII-I, 1973, 25-29.

Harper, Edward, P., 'Social Consequences of an Unsuccessful Low Caste Movement (ed James Silverberg), *Social Mobility in the Caste System in India,* Mounton, The Hague 1968, 36-65.

Heer, David M., *Society and Population*, Prentice-Hall of India, New Delhi 1978.

Hegan, Everett E., *On the Theory of Social Change: How Economic Growth Begins*, Dorsey Press, Homewood, Illinois 1962.

Hurd, John II, 'The Economic Consequences of Indirect Rule in India', *The Indian Economic and Social History Review,* Vol XII-2, 1975, 169-82.

Jones, Kenneth W., *Arya Dharm: Hindu Consciousness in the Nineteenth Century Punjab*, Manohar, Delhi 1976.

———, *Socio-Religious Movements in India*, Cambridge University Press, Cambridge 1990.

Juergensmeyer, Mark, *Religion As Social Vision: The Movement Against Untouchability in 20th Century Punjab*, University of California Press, Berkeley 1982.

Kessinger, Tom G., *Vilyatpur (1848-1968): Social and Economic Change in a North Indian Village,* University of California, Berkeley 1974.

———, 'Sources for the Social and Economic History of Rural Punjab', (ed W. Eric Gustafson and Kenneth W. Jones), *Sources on Punjab History*, Manohar Book Service, Delhi 1975, 9-44.

———, 'Regional Economy 1757-1857' (ed Dharma Kumar), *The Cambridge Economic History of India*, Vol 2, Cambridge University Press, Cambridge 1983, 242-69.

Khanna, J.S., 'Lagging Industrial Development in the Punjab', *PSE Economic Analyst*, Vol II, 1980, 83-125.

Khosla, G.S., 'The Growth of the Railway System in the Punjab', *The Panjab Past and Present: Essays in Honour of Dr. Ganda Singh*, Punjabi University, Patiala 1976.

Krishnamurthy, J., 'Changing Concepts of Work in Indian Censuses, 1901-61', *The Indian Economic and Social History Review*, Vol XIV- 3, 1977, 323-40.

———, 'Changes in the Composition of the Work Force in Manufacturing Industry in India, 1901-51', *The Indian Economic and Social History Review,* Vol VI, 1969.

Kulkarni, A.R., 'Presidential Address: Servants of Village Communities in Maharashtra', *Proceedings Punjab History Conference*, Patiala 1980, 11-22.

———, 'Presidential Address: An Indian Village', *Indian History Congress* 1992.

Lasswell, Thomas E., *Class and Stratum: An Introduction to Concepts and Research,* Houghton Mifflin Company, New York 1965.

Lavan, Spencer, *Ahmadiyah Movement: A History and Perspective,* Manohar, Delhi 1974.

Lewis, Oscar, *Village Life in Northern India*, University of Illinois Press, Urbana 1958.

Lohelin, C.H., 'History of Christian Missions in the Punjab', *The Panjab Past and Present,* Vol VII-I, 1973, 186-89.

Lucas, E.D., *The Economic Life of a Punjab Village,* Civil and Military Gazette Press, Lahore nd.

Lynch, Owen M., *The Politics of Untouchability: Social Mobility and Social Change in a City of India*, Columbia University Press, New York 1969.

Malik, Ikram Ali, *A Bibliography of the Punjab and its Dependencies 1848-1910*, Historical Research Society of Pakistan, Lahore 1978.

Mandelbaum, David G., *Society in India*, Popular Prakashan, Bombay 1970.

Maheshwari, B.P., *Industrial and Agricultural Development of India Since 1914,* S.Chand and Co., New Delhi 1971.

Marenco, Ethne, K., *The Transformation of Sikh Society,* Heritage Publishers, New Delhi 1976.

Mathur, Y.B., *British Administration of the Punjab (1849-1875),* Surjit Book Depot, Delhi nd.

Maya Singh, *The Punjabi Dictionary*, Languages Department Punjab, Patiala 1972 (first published 1895).

Mcleod, W.H., *Punjabis in New Zealand*, GNDU, Amritsar 1986.

Mitra, Asok, *India's Population: Aspects of Quality and Control,* Abhinav Publication, 2 vols. New Delhi 1975.

Morris, D. Morris, Toru Matsui, Bipan Chandra and T. Roy Choudhri, *Indian Economy in the Nineteenth Century: A Symposium,* Indian Economic and Social History Association, Delhi School of Economic, Delhi 1969.

Newell, Richard, 'The Census as a Tool in the Study of Modern Urban Labour Force in India: A case Study of Tamilnadu' (ed Norman G. Barrier), *The Census in British India*, Manohar Publications, New Delhi 1981, 175-225.

O'Malley, L.S.S., *Indian Caste Customs*, Vikas Publishing House, New Delhi 1974.

Om Parkash, *A Statistical Analysis of the Economic Conditions of Peasants in the Punjab 1939-49*, Ludhiana 1950.

Raj, K.N. and others (ed), *Essays on Commercialization of Indian Agriculture,* OUP, Delhi 1985.

Rao, M.S.A., *Social Movements and Social Transformation in India*, Manohar, Delhi 1987.

Ravinder Kumar, *Western India in the Nineteenth Century: A Study of Social History of Maharashtra*, Routledge and Kegan Paul, London 1968.

———, 'State and Society in Modern India', *Bhartiya Samajik Chintan,* Vol VII: 1-4, 1984, 25-40.

Row, William L., 'Caste, Kinship and Association in Urban India' (ed Aiden South Hall), *Urban Anthropology,* OUP, New York 1973, 211-50.

Saberwal, Satish, *Mobile Men: Limits of Social Change in Urban Punjab,* Vikas Publishing House, New Delhi 1976.

———, 'Receding Pollution: Inter-caste Relations in Urban Punjab', *Sociological Bulletin,* 22, 1973, 59-77.

———, 'Status and Entrepreneurship: The Case of Ramgarhias' (eds M.N. Srinivas and Others), *Dimensions of Social Change in India*, Allied Publishers, Bombay 1978, 155-68.

Sachchidanand, 'Social Change in India-A Historical Perspective' (eds K.S. Mathur and Others), *Studies in Social Change,* Ethnographic and Folk Culture Society, U.P., Lucknow 1973, 53-68.

Saini, B.S. *The Social and Economic History of the Punjab (1901-1939)*, Ess Ess Publications, Delhi 1975.

Sarkar, Sumit, *Modern India 1885-1947,* Macmillan, N. Delhi 1983.

Scott, Joan, 'Urban and Rural Artisans in 19th Century France', *The Journal of Economic History,* Vol XXXVII, No. I, March 1977.

Sharma, Harish Chander, 'Demographic Distribution of the Artisans of the Punjab in the late Nineteenth Century: Some Problems and Prospects', *Proceedings Punjab History Conference Patiala 1978,* 147-53.

———, 'Expressions of Caste Mobility Among the Artisans of the Punjab', *Proceedings Punjab History Conference Patiala 1979,* 252- 57.

———, 'Artisans in the Punjab (1849-1947): Occupational Change and New Social Relations', *Journal of Regional History,* Vol I, 1980, 107-119.

———, 'Politicization of the Chamars: Early 20th Century Punjab', *Journal of Regional History,* Vol IV, 1983, 128-38.

———, 'A Note on Urban Artisans of the Punjab', *Proceedings Indian History Congress 1983*, 556-62.

Sharma K.L., 'Downward Social Mobility: Some Observations', *Sociological Bulletin*, 22, 1973, 59-77.

Sharma K.N., *Institutions, Networks and Social Change*, Indian Institute of Advanced Study, Shimla nd.

Sharma, Radha, 'Agrarian Structure of Amritsar and Lahore During Early Nineteenth Century' (eds J.S. Grewal and Indu Banga), *Maharaja Ranjit Singh and His Times,* GNDU, Amritsar 1980, 169-76.

———, 'Social Configuration in Three Parganas under Sikh Rule', *The Panjab Past and Present,* Vol XXIII-I, 1989, 81-86.

Sidhu, Sharda, *A Study of Fertility and Physique in the Scheduled Caste Women of Punjab with special Reference to Age Changes*, Ph. D. Thesis, Punjabi University, Patiala 1982.

Silverberg, James (ed), *Social Mobility in the Caste System of India*, Mounton, The Hague 1968.

Singer, Milton (ed), *Traditional India: Structure and Change,* Rawat Publications, Jaipur 1975.

Smith, Anthony, D., *Social Change: Social Theory and Historical Perspective,* Longmans, London 1976.

Smith, Raymond T., 'Some Social Characteristics of Indian Immigrants to British Guiana', *Population Studies*, Vol XIII-I, 1959-60, 34-39.

Srinivas, M.N., (ed), *India's Villages,* Asia Publishing House, New York 1960.

———, *Social Change in Modern India,* Orient Paperback, New Delhi 1977 (first published 1968).

Srivastava, H.S., *The History of Indian Famines,* Sri Ram Mehra, Agra 1968.

Steingass, F., *A Comprehensive Persian-English Dictionary,* Oriental Books Reprint, New Delhi 1973.

Tandon, Parkash, *Punjabi Century (1857-1947)*, Chatto and Windus, London 1961.

Theodorson, George A., Theodorson, Achilles G., *A Modern Dictionary of Sociology*, Methuen & Co., London 1969.

Thorburn, S.S., *The Punjab in Peace and War,* Languages Department Punjab, Patiala 1970 (first published 1883).

Triandis, Harry C., 'The Impact of Social Change on Attitudes' (ed

Bert T. King and Elliot Mcginneir), *Attitudes and Social Change,* Academic Press, New York 1972, 127-34.

Tumin, Melvin M., *Caste in a Peasant Society,* Princeton, New Jersey 1952.

Tyagi, A.R., *The Civil Service in a Developing Society*, Sterling Publishers, Delhi 1969.

Vashishtha, Vijay Kumar, 'Bhagat Movement Among the Tribals in Southern Rajasthan 1907-1948', paper presented at a Review Meeting of the *Project on Socio-Religious Movements and Cultural Net Works in Indian Civilization* at Indian Institute of Advanced Study, Shimla in May 1992 (Mimeographed).

Webster, John C.B., *The Christian Community and Change in Nineteenth Century North India*, The Macmillian Company, Delhi 1976.

Wilson, H.H., *A Glossary of Judicial and Revenue Terms and of Useful Words Occuring in Official Documents Relating to the Administration of the Government of British India*, Munshi Ram Manohar Lal, Delhi 1968 (first published 1885).

Yogendra Singh, *Social Stratification and Change in India,* Manohar Book Service, Delhi 1977.

Young, P.V., *Scientific Social Surveys and Research,* Prentice- Hall India, New Delhi 1975.

Zacharia, K.C., *A Historical Study of Internal Migration in the Indian Sub-Continent,* Asia Publishing House, New York 1964.

Index